Margot Bittner

Enhancing the Fusion Method to Fusion_B

Margot Bittner

Enhancing the Fusion Method to Fusion_B

Requirements Engineering and Formal Specification

VDM Verlag Dr. Müller

Imprint

Bibliographic information by the German National Library: The German National Library lists this publication at the German National Bibliography; detailed bibliographic information is available on the Internet at http://dnb.d-nb.de.

Cover image: www.purestockx.com

Publisher:
VDM Verlag Dr. Müller Aktiengesellschaft & Co. KG , Dudweiler Landstr. 125 a, 66123 Saarbrücken, Germany,
Phone +49 681 9100-698, Fax +49 681 9100-988,
Email: info@vdm-verlag.de

Zugl.: Berlin, TU Berlin, D83, 2005

Produced in USA and UK by:
Lightning Source Inc., La Vergne, Tennessee, USA
Lightning Source UK Ltd., Milton Keynes, UK
BookSurge LLC, 5341 Dorchester Road, Suite 16, North Charleston, SC 29418, USA

ISBN: 978-3-639-00818-0

Table of Contents

III   The Extensions of Fusion/UML   85

7   Enhancement – Determining Requirements   89

8   Enhancement — Towards Formal Specification   105

9   *Fusion$_B$* – The Extended Fusion/UML Method   123

List of Figures

Foreword

As the title indicates, the present book focuses on extensions to an existing software engineering method. The book's structure and the terminology used betray its origin as a doctoral thesis, but it is a great deal more than a mere supplement to existing material on the subject.

The book offers a detailed and comprehensive study of the software engineering method *Fusion*, which has been successful over the past fifteen years. Though well established, the term *software engineering method* requires further elucidation. It refers to methods used for software production - in other words: the industrial software development process.

As the name Fusion suggests, the method was initially designed by an English group at Imperial College London and Hewlett-Packard to *fuse* existing ideas on software analysis, design, specification and programming and develop them conceptually and notationally into consistent models reflecting the state of the art. It has since been attempted to integrate into Fusion new ideas on the structuring of software and the software development process resulting from a so-called paradigm change in research: the object-oriented view of the software product and process, the emergence of new object-oriented specification languages and the elaboration of the eminently important field of requirements engineering, to mention just some of them.

The present book traces the path taken by the author, as a member of the Technical University of Berlin's Software Engineering Group, in developing the substantial extensions she has made to the method. It was an arduous and thorny path that took at least ten years to negotiate: Fusion/UML was the focus of the Software Engineering course, a well-established component of the computer science programme at the Technical University of Berlin. Hundreds of students have not only had to study this method; they have tested and critically evaluated its practicability in extensive project work and in their degree theses. Special thanks are due, then, to our students: without their input - almost invariably reflecting their initial scepticism but very often culminating in their enthusiastic approval - it would have taken us much longer to reach our destination. Of course, further changes and additions (or omissions) are still conceivable, but whether these are conducive to Fusion in terms of the method's acceptance and stability is questionable, to say the least.

Readers will notice that Fusion consists of a set of mutually attuned models that map out the path from the initial idea for a software system to its final implementation. Here, the principle of abstraction - inherent to all scientific work - has been heeded throughout. It is one of the lessons learned from the so-called software crisis of the 1960s that ever more complex software applications cannot simply be mastered by equally complex, notationally overloaded means of description. Which is why Fusion models are characterized not so much by a wealth of modelling elements but rather by gradual reduction of such elements as the project progresses. The inability to work, at a specific time and point in the development process, on details that might the obscure the view of the product under development is a well-considered application of the principle of abstraction and an intentional feature of Fusion.

Having accompanied Margot Bittner's work for over ten years, I share her view that we need to warn against researchers' repeated efforts to push one single idea, one single language, one single method, which then balloons and eventually becomes rigid and inflexible. Thus, while UML represents a highly laudable attempt to develop a semantically sound language set, trying to derive from it a *universal method* is an extremely dubious - if not dangerous - undertaking. I hope that this book enjoys the success it deserves and that readers who are personally involved in the business of software engineering will find it stimulating and insightful.

Wilfried Koch, June 2008

Chapter 1

Introduction

To obtain a more precise grasp of what software is, we must first view it as the non-material product of human creative effort. Software is a well-defined *abstract*: only by reducing the requirements of the real world and by tailoring the functionality of the computer system are tangible models produced. The construction of software is a process of continuous model building. Its aim is to arrive at an interpretation of the resulting models. This interpretation can be carried out by tools or persons, by either the transformation or mapping of models. In any case, it is the definition of relationships between different models. Software is always the implementation of models into reality (possibly a virtual reality), and thus into a new reality of computer embedment [GKJ95].

What does implementation mean? Three aspects are always mentioned:

1. Architecture Aspect
   Software is implemented using an adequate description of programs, data elements and data structures. The structure of a program is the prerequisite for understanding the underlying functional models of software and their possible translation into interpreting code. The structure of data – the data model – is essential for every possible application (manipulation). What the appropriate descriptions are, needs to be defined in detail. This is not a simple question. It leads us to the essence of software[Bro95], and to the specific problems of software engineering

2. Document Aspect
   The physical representation of software is a set of various documents. They differ in their intended use or are written (modelled) for different users of the software.

3. Execution Aspect
   Software is implemented in programs (i.e. a set of instructions that cor-

3

responds to execution), whose interpretation is transformed through the hardware of the modelled functionality of a computer system.

In software engineering, the emphasis is on the creation of *methods* for constructing software systems. A method should give us a recipe guiding the process of software construction – henceforth this is called the software process and it addresses the problem of designing a software system. In order to construct the "right" software system – one with which the customer and the developer is satisfied – a correct understanding of the domain to be modelled is needed. In the software development process, the first step towards this goal is to define the requirements for the system. The process of finding the requirements, classifying them and verifying them against all models created throughout the software process is one aim in creating a better system. A better system is one that is less erroneous and more reliable for the users and the environment in which the system is deployed. Another task, just as important as the one mentioned above, is the formal specification of the system to be built. In order to perform these tasks, a method is needed to assist and guide the developers in building good systems in their process of software development.

The thesis focuses on extending the existing Fusion method [BK00] in requirements engineering and formal specification, and in particular integrating the formal object-oriented specification language Object Z [DR00, Smi00]. This can be seen as one of the most important developments in the area of systematic software development to produce reliable software.

1.1   Background

Fusion [Cea94] is a method for analyzing, designing and implementing object-oriented software systems. It has contributed to the development of the Unified Modeling Language (UML)[OMG99]. We use a combination of UML and Fusion models with the Fusion process in teaching and project work [BK00].

This method, called Fusion/UML[1] consists of a relatively fixed process divided into two subprocesses: analysis and design. It defines consistency rules for all models of the two subprocesses, enabling it to control consistency *in* the various models and *between* them throughout the development process. The final result of the Fusion/UML process is an accurate description of the class interfaces, suitable for any object-oriented programming language.

This analysis process looks at the system from the user's point of view, suggesting

---

[1]Objektorientierte Analyse und Design, Die Fusion-Methode unter Verwendung von UML was developed at the Technische Universität Berlin in 1999 [BK01] in this thesis we refer to it as Fusion/UML.

how the user or system intends to interact with the system. The result of the first part of the method, analysis, is a so-called *Operation Model* describing the system operations in schematic form. Although still part of the analysis, the Operation Model looks at the functionality of the system in some detail. Thus it might well be considered a model that is somewhere between analysis and design. It gives the Fusion method its appeal of seamlessness. Seamlessness is one of the attributes always emphasized by object orientation. There is thus no need to distinguish between analysis and design. Here, with this method, you can actually see the distinction.

The most constructive task is producing a set of object interaction graphs (*Object Interaction Model*), known in UML as collaboration graphs. They define the system operations by means of message flows (method invocation) between objects in the system. Analysis and design contain various other models, but the two parts *Operation Model* and *Object Interaction Model* contain most of the information about the operational part of the system design.

There follows a brief description of Fusion/UML as it has been developed and used successfully in many case studies in teaching and research.

1.2 Current Situation

The existing Fusion/UML method assumes that requirements elicitation has already been completed and that the requirements document exists in the form of a problem description. The process of eliciting, analyzing and checking requirements has been done and the result of this process is the problem description. This has implications for further development steps in the software development process:

- Important information is lost because extracting requirements from the problem description for further use is not part of the method.

- There is no checking between the problem description and the requirements description and their further use in all the method's models.

If we consider existing software development process models [Som01, Pre01], like the *Waterfall*, *V-Model* or *Spiral Model*, it is clear that the validation of the developed system and its requirements is necessary. Indeed, each model developed during the software process must be validated against its requirements. To get to the point of validation, we first have to obtain the source that can be used to validate the products or documents: The process establishing the services the system should provide and the constraints under which it must operate is called *requirements engineering*.

The requirements process [KS97, SS97] comprises activities such as elicitation, analysis, negotiation and documentation, the demand being that a requirements process should be seamlessly integrated into the existing Fusion process. The Fusion method builds on the natural problem description. This description is not sufficient to enable us to understand the problem domain and the task of developing and implementing the software system. An adjusted process model for gathering, classifying and formally describing requirements is needed.

Methods may be designed only for a certain part of the life cycle and must therefore be supplemented by other techniques to cover the whole life cycle. Formal methods have often been limited in their coverage of the software life cycle.

Formal methods for software systems are based on mathematical results such as logic and algebra, which give these methods a sound semantical model. Formal methods can supplement less formal methods used in the overall system development process. They could be used not instead of but in addition to informal or semiformal methods. So far, formal methods have proved useful in specification and verification. It is worth exploring how they can be used in requirements analysis, refinement and testing.

Specification is one aspect of the overall process of developing software systems. Formal specification is the process of creating precise models based on mathematical notation and the semantics of a proposed system. The purpose of formal specification is to create a description of the system's functionality that has a sound mathematical basis.

Since no one method is likely to be suitable for describing and analyzing every aspect of a complex system, a pragmatic approach is to use different methods in combination.

The smooth integration of the formal specification into the Fusion process is – like the requirements process – one of the challenges addressed here.

1.3   Aim

If we look at the graphical representations of the overall Fusion process, we notice that the problem description is either depicted as a large cloud or it does not exist at all. This means that the requirements process as such is not part of the method itself. Our aim is to clearly structure the cloud. This structure will enable us to identify requirements activities that can be transferred to and integrated into the method. We will see that this approach contributes to all subsequent activities of the method. We will demonstrate how requirements determination will have an impact on extension of the formal specification. Formal statements, one of the results of requirements determination, are candidates for class and environmental invariants. Environmental invariants are important for the preconditions of system state and system operations.

Our aim in this book is to show that it is possible to integrate the requirements determination and the formal specification into an existing object-oriented development method. New modelling elements are designed and integrated into the notation. The process steps of the method are modified, reflecting all models of the process.

We focus on the two main areas of the software development process that are not covered by the Fusion/UML method:

1. the integration of requirements engineering

2. the integration of a formal method

Both requirements engineering and formal methods are very important activities in software development. Formal specification cannot be justified without some form of requirements engineering. We believe that extending this method will improve the analysis phase, and with it the next phases in the software development process. It is important to integrate the two activities in such a way that they fit smoothly into the method process and also incorporate the model's elements. The information gathered during requirements determination is used in the subsequent models of analysis. During the process of requirements determination, requirements are defined in a formal way. These requirements are suitable for use as environmental invariants or class invariants of the formal description. Here, we see that information gained in the early part of analysis is used in the next phase of the method. The formal specification is developed from the operation model and the object interaction model and is enriched through the INIT operation and the class invariants of the requirements definition.

1.4 Organization of the book

The book is divided into three parts. The first part, consisting of Chapters 2, 3 and 4, reflects the three disciplines in which this work is embedded – software engineering,requirements engineering and formal methods. The current Fusion method, which is dealt with in Part II (Chapters 5 and 6) of this book, forms the basis for the enhancement. The third and last part comprises the remaining chapters and includes the main work: the two extensions to the method, the change to the Fusion method, a comparison with other derivations of Fusion and the book's conclusion.

Part I
Chapter 2 gives a historical overview of software engineering and its modelling

from the early sixties up to the present. With the von Neumann architecture that reflected modelling at that time – the data flow diagram – it encompasses the abstraction of procedures and also the abstract data to abstract data types, modular decomposition and the software production process. The chapter ends with a synopsis of the role of methods in software engineering.

Chapter 3 focuses on requirements engineering, one of the disciplines of software development engineering. It gives a summary of what requirements engineering is, describing the process and its phases. In particular, it deals with those phases that are part of the new Fusion process.

The next chapter deals with formal specification. Here, as in Chapter 2, a historical overview is given, this time of formal specification and formal development methods. Special attention is given to Z and Object-Z. This topic is also part of the enhancement of Fusion.

Chapters 2, 3 and 4 give an overview of the three disciplines on which this book is based: software engineering, requirements engineering and formal specification. They are designed to give the reader an idea of how large and broad the context of the book is. Very little of what has been written about these disciplines is included here, but we believe it is important for understanding the present book.

Part II

In Chapters 5 and 6, the Fusion Method/UML as taught by the Software Engineering research group is explained. Since Fusion was introduced into teaching, several modifications have been made to the method, one of which is the adaption of the graphical diagrams to UML notation. We use the modification made by [BK00] as a starting point for our enhancement.

Part III

The foundations having been laid, we go on, in Chapter 7 to present the extension to the method, Requirements Determination. This chapter describes the determination of the domains of the application domain and outlines the extraction and classification of the requirements and non-responsible statements. Throughout the process, we are sensitive to links to other method artefacts for tracing requirements and consistency checks.

Chapter 8 deals with the integration of the formal specification into the method as well as the use of Object Z for checking consistency between the Operation Model and the Object Interaction Model. This activity yields Object-Z classes that are complemented by class invariants from the requirements description and initialization operations.

Chapter 9 includes the two extensions to the new method, resulting in its new name $Fusion_B$. It presents the new process, the models and the consistency.

The penultimate chapter draws a comparison between the new $Fusion_B$ and derivations of the original Fusion method in the area of requirements engineering and formal specification.

The last chapter gives a summary of the results and a self-assessment of the work done as well as suggesting future developments.

The appendix contains the Case Study as well as the syntactical description of the method's models using EBNF, the graphical notation of the modelling elements, and offers an outlook on how requirements templates for tools might be designed.

Part I

The Foundation

The key of using abstraction effectively in [analysing, designing and] programming is to find a notion of relevance for both the builder of the abstraction and the user of the abstraction. And that is the true art of building systems.

John V. Guttag[Gut01]

Chapter 2

Software Engineering and Modelling

Historically, the term software engineering was introduced in 1968 [NR69], when the poor prospects for developing high-quality software on time and within the budget became apparent. Developers were unable to set the right goals, estimate the resources required to attain those goals or manage the expectations and the needs of customers.

The problem of building and delivering software systems on time is still an important research issue. The blame has variously been put on customers who do not know what they want, on the "soft" elements of software engineering or on the discipline's youth. What is the problem then?

Complexity and change are the answer. Both are properties pointed to by Brooks [Bro87, Bro95]. Software engineering is and will continue to be a modelling activity.

In this chapter, the development of software engineering is described from its early days up to present. Then we give a brief description of the software development process. The chapter ends with an outline of the role the methods play in the software engineering process.

2.1   A Historical Look at Software Engineering

Those who cannot remember the past are condemned to repeat it.

George Santayana[San05]

The history of software engineering is characterized by the development of tools for solving ever more complex problems. Such tools can be used to produce software, which is more than simply editing or compiling. One feature of advances in programming languages and tools has been the continuous increase in the level of abstraction.

Influenced by the von Neumann hardware architecture, solutions at a low level of abstraction were only applicable to small problems. Software was written in machine language. Programmers entered instructions and data individually and explicitly into the computer memory, one instruction at a time. The realization that memory layout and the updating of references could be automated and that symbolic names could be used for operation codes and memory addresses led to the development of the symbolic assembler. The substitution of simple symbols for machine operation code, machine addresses and sequences of instructions (macros) was probably the first form of abstraction in software.

The development of notations, tools and methods for producing software was needed to deal with the growing number of ever more complex problems, and conversely the existence of tools enabled increasingly complex problems to be solved.

It became clear that certain patterns of operations, e.g. arithmetic expressions, were generally appropriate. It was possible to create these patterns automatically from a mathematics-like notation. These were patterns for the evaluation of arithmetic expressions, for procedure invocation and for loops and conditional statements. They were found in programming languages like Fortran and Cobol. This concept is known as *structured programming.* . Higher-level languages allowed the development of more complex programs. The next step on the path to higher abstraction was the separation of data and operations.

The introduction of procedural concepts made it possible to have separate compilable units – the abstraction of subroutines.

The next abstraction step came with the introduction of procedures as part of the concept of a separate data space. The concept of block structure and scope, as defined in Algol60, made it possible to distinguish between global and local scope of data. Another important concept on the path to abstraction was the mathematical notion of recursion, applied to the world of programming languages.

Next came the extension of the type concept from basic types, as in Fortran and Cobol, to data structures such as arrays and records and their constructors.

Pascal and its successors introduced the weak and strong abstraction of types and the type concept.

Advances in language design continued with the introduction of modules to provide protection for related procedures and data structures, with the separation of a module's specification from implementation (i.e. Modula2) and the introduction of abstract data types. The concept of abstract data types was based on a theory that involved an understanding of the software structure, specification expressed as abstract models or algebraic axioms, language issues like modules, scopes and user-defined types, the integrity of the result (invariants of data structures and protection from other manipulation), rules for combining types and information hiding (protection of properties not explicitly included in specifications).

Further concepts for abstraction in programming were the class concept (Simula67) and instantiation in object orientation (Smalltalk, Eiffel) and design patterns. On a higher level of abstraction, the architecture pattern and software components were introduced. The abstraction of programming went from algorithms to system solution.

The abstraction led from problem domain to system solution and that was the beginning of *analysis and design*. During the 1970s, many design methods were created to address the growing complexity of software. The most influential of them was top-down structured design, but the data-driven approach also had a considerable impact. In the data-driven method, the structure of the system is derived by mapping system inputs to outputs.

All notations were integrated in unified methods, e.g. OMT and Booch [RBP+91, Boo94] which consisted in describing an abstraction concept of models with their modelling elements and the process of combining those models. There are a number of different methods for putting the real world and the virtual world on hardware. On a higher level of abstraction, the hardware is a machine interpreter like Java Enterprise, etc. The virtual world implements an abstraction of the real world, e.g. a person as an identifier, depending on the problem to be solved.

Attempts are currently being made to define a unified modelling language (UML) and a unified modelling process (UMP). Whether this attempt is successful will be evident in a few years' time.

2.2 Software Development Process

The software development process defines activities and organizational procedures to enhance collaboration within the development team so that a quality product is delivered to the customers.

The term software process describes a process used to develop computer software. It may be an *ad hoc* process, devised by the team for one single project. However, the term often refers to a standardized, documented methodology that has been used before on similar projects or one that is used habitually within an organization (cf. Capability Maturity Model(CMM) [SEI95]).

Managers who are held accountable for software development may look for common features in the efforts of their organizations. If these managers are process-oriented, (rather than people-oriented, task-oriented, profit-oriented, project-oriented, etc.), they may seek methodologies or other substitutes that can serve as templates for the software development process.

Of course, it is entirely rational for other – non-process-oriented – managers to use a documented software development process or methodology. In such cases, one might say that the methodology is used by them as a substitute for the set of process-oriented skills required in any software engineering project.

There are many different software processes, but the following fundamental activities are common to them all:

- Requirements analysis
  The system requirements must be discovered from the application domain by all stakeholders in the system to be built.

- Software specification The system functionality and the constraints must be specified unequivocally.

- Software design and implementation
  The software must meet the specification.

- Software validation
  The software must be validated in terms of its requirements to ensure that it meets the customer's needs.

- Software evolution
  The software must evolve to meet changing customer needs.

2.3   The Role of Methods in Software Engineering

Methods play a key role in any engineering discipline. One could argue that engineering can not exist without methods. The problems confronting engineers are so complex and new that some kind of guidelines are needed to solve them. The quality of a software engineering process depends strongly on the quality of the method used. But it also depends on the type of system being built. There are several types of systems: information systems, embedded or interactive systems, real-time systems, control systems, to name only the most common ones.

A software engineering method is a structured approach to software development whose aim is to facilitate the production of high-quality software in a cost-effective way. In the late 1970s and early 1980s, the first methods such as Structured Analysis [Dem79] and Jackson System Development (JSD) [Jac83] became available. The idea was to identify the basic functional components of a system. These function-oriented methods are still in use today. In the late 1980s and 1990s, these approaches were complemented by the object-oriented methods introduced by Booch [Boo94] and Raumbaugh [Boo94]. In the late 1990s, the emphasis shifted to methods for software components [Szy98, BK01]. Today, the focus is on aspect orientation [Fea05].

All these methods are based on the idea of developing models of a system, which may be represented graphically, semiformally or formally, and using these models as a system specification or design. There is no one ideal method, and different methods are suitable for different areas. Object-oriented methods are more appropriate for interactive and certain kinds of embedded systems, but not for systems with real-time constraints.

Formal methods can supplement less formal methods in the overall system development process. They can be used not instead of but in addition to informal or semiformal methods. So far, formal methods have shown their strength in specification and verification. It is worthwhile exploring how they can be used in *requirements analysis, refinement and testing.*

Requirements analysis deals with the customers' – often imprecise – idea of what they want. Formal methods can help customers and developers to define precise system requirements.

Refinement is the opposite of verification. It is the process of taking one level of specification (or implementation) and, by a series of correctness-preserving transformations, synthesizing a lower-level specification or implementation.

Testing is one of the most costly items in all software projects. Formal methods can play a role in the validation process, e.g. using formal specifications to generate test suites and using model- or proof-checking tools to determine relationships between specifications and test suites, and test suites and code.

Chapter 3

Requirements Engineering

Requirements engineering is the branch of software engineering concerned with the real-world goals for, functions of, and constraints on software systems. It is also concerned with relationship of these factors to precise specifications of software behaviour, and to their evolution over time and across software families.

Pamela Zave[Zav97]

It has long been established that the effectiveness and flexibility of a software product is strongly dependent on getting the requirements right. In this chapter, we describe the process of Requirements engineering and its result. We give some definitions of the term *requirement*, then classify requirements and list some different types of requirements. We then go on to look at the requirements engineering process, focusing on those activities that are supported by the new method called *Fusion$_B$* . Finally, we give a brief summary of the chapter.

3.1   Introduction

There have been problems with the development of software systems since the 1960s. Too many systems have been delivered too late and over budget. One of the reasons for this was the poorly performed requirements process in software development. This was given little attention by software developers. In recent years, the information technology industry has recognized the importance of requirements engineering, particularly requirements management.

3.2   What is Requirements Engineering?

> The hardest single part of building a software system is deciding precisely what to build. No other part of the conceptual work is as difficult as establishing the detailed technical requirements. No other part of the work so cripples the resulting system if done wrong. No other part is as difficult to rectify later.

Fred Brooks wrote this in 1987 [Bro87] and little has changed since then [Dav93, Fau97]. The inability to produce complete, correct, and unambiguous software requirements is still considered the major cause of software failure today [TD97].

In [LK95], we find the following definition of the term requirements engineering: "The systematic process of developing requirements through an iterative co-operative process of analysing the problem, documenting the resulting observations in a variety of representation formats, and checking the accuracy of the understanding gain."

Requirements engineering emphasizes the utilization of systematic and repeatable techniques that ensure the completeness, consistency and relevance of the system requirements [Som01]. Specifically, requirements engineering encompasses elicitation, analysis, specification, verification and management:

- Requirements elicitation is the process of discovering, reviewing, documenting and understanding the user's needs and constraints with respect to the system.

- Requirements analysis is the process of refining the user's needs and constraints.

- Requirements specification is the process of documenting the user's needs and constraints clearly and precisely.

- Requirements verification is the process of ensuring that the system requirements are complete, correct, consistent, and clear.

- Requirements management is the process of scheduling, coordinating, and documenting the requirements engineering activities (i.e. elicitation, analysis, specification and verification) [TD97].

Requirements engineering is complex because of the three roles involved in producing even a single requirement: the *user or customer*, the *developer* (who designs and implements the system), and the *analyst* (who analyzes and documents the requirements). Typically, the user or customer understands the problem to be solved by the system, but not *how* to develop the system. The developer understands the tools and techniques required to construct and maintain the system, but not the problem to *be solved* by the system. The analyst needs to create a statement that communicates less ambiguously to the developer what the user wants. Requirements addresses a fundamental communication problem.

This communication problem is further compounded by the number and diversity of users. In practice, any stakeholder has needs and expectations (i.e. requirements) with respect to the system. A stakeholder is a role played by any of the various people or systems involved in or affected by system development. This includes executives who know the organization's business goals and constraints; end users who know how the products will be used; marketers who know the market demands; technical managers who know the available personnel; and developers who know the available tools and technology. Successful requirements engineering depends on the identification and solicitation of the appropriate community of stakeholders.

Requirements are pervasive, continuously affecting all development and maintenance phases of a system's growing process by providing primary information needed by those phases. The requirements constitute a trigger mechanism for software development and maintenance. Testing, for instance, depends on a precise statement of quality and behavioural requirements in order to define the standard of correctness against which to test. Requirements engineering is not just an up-front activity, but rather has ramifications over the entire software development and maintenance process.

The longer the system's lifetime, the more it is exposed to changes in requirements resulting from changes in the needs and concerns of the stakeholders. For example, the end user's demands can change as a result of new features offered by competing organization's products. The organization's business goals and constraints can change as a result of market demands, new laws or new insurance regulations. New technologies and software tools such as operating systems can change the way the system is constructed. Mechanisms are needed for managing the changes, i.e. a requirements change management process – a process based on the traceability links between the requirements and the system.

3.2.1 Requirements Artefacts

First of all, the requirements artefacts produced by requirements engineering are important core assets in their own right. Beyond that, requirements engineering creates requirements that feed the development and acquisition of other core assets. Requirements artefacts help to:

1. Determine the feasibility and refine the scope of the system. The initial

version of the use case is frequently based on an informal notion of the application environment. Requirements engineering refines the scope, and hence the business case, by determining more precisely the requirements for the system.

2. Lay the groundwork for the software architecture.

3. Ensure that the other core assets support it.

4. Create the test cases and other test artefacts.

A significant difference in requirements engineering involves a rapid initial parsing of the requirements for key stakeholders to initiate early design work, capturing the high-level requirements that affect the initial design (i.e. the architecturally significant requirements [Jac99]). The purpose of this is to minimize the time to initial delivery and to demonstrate the feasibility and establish the credibility of the product line approach. In short, to provide an early justification of the investment [Gra98].

3.3 The Role of Requirements Engineering

Requirements engineering plays a key role in:

- determining the feasibility of producing a particular product, namely the system or product

- validating, testing and deploying the system

Requirements play a role in these activities. This is the primary mechanism for the evolution of software over time.

Determining the feasibility of a particular product is an ongoing activity that is part of building a business case for that product. The initial version of the product is frequently based on an informal description of the prospective product. Requirements engineering, particularly elicitation and analysis, supports the business case for the product by determining more precisely the requirements for that product. Requirements analysis determines domain requirements, system requirements and statements for which the system is not responsible.

3.4 What are Requirements?

In the previous section on requirements engineering, we outlined the requirements engineering process, the techniques to capture requirements as well as testing, tracing and versioning. But what are requirements?

Merriam Webster's Collegiate Dictionary gives the following definitions of requirements[Web93]:

a: Something required, something wanted or needed.

b: Something essential to the existence or occurrence of something else.

For software engineering, requirements could be defined as follows:

- from the perspective of a customer: what a customer needs, wants or expects

- from the perspective of a software developer: what a software developer analyzes, designs and implements and which should ultimately work according to requirements.

Requirements are statements of what the system must do, how it must behave, the properties it must exhibit, the qualities it must possess, and the constraints that the system and its development must satisfy. IEEE defines a requirement as:

1. a condition or capability needed by a user to solve a problem or achieve an objective

2. a condition or capability that must be met or possessed by a system or system component to satisfy a contract, standard, specification, or other formally imposed document

3. a documented representation of a condition or capability as in definition 1. or 2. [oEE90]

Michael Jackson defines requirements in [Jac95] as follows: "Requirements are about the *phenomena of the application domain*, not about the machine. To describe them exactly, we describe the required relationship among the phenomena of the problem context. But not all the phenomena of the problem context are shared with the machine."

Jackson and Zave [ZJ97] define *requirements on the basis of statements* [Jac95]. Statements which have optative properties are statement about the environment: how the system should be when it is linked to the environment. Statements about the environment which have indicative properties are assumptions or knowledge about the environment.

Davis[Dav93] distinguishes between *behavioural requirements* and *nonbehavioural requirements*.Behavioral requirements are those requirements that specify the inputs (stimuli) to the system, the output (responses) from the system and the behavioural relationships between them. They are also known as functional or operational requirements. On the other hand, nonbehavioural requirements are requirements that describe the required overall attributes of the system, including portability, reliability, efficiency, human engineering, testability and modification.

Loucopoulos and Karakostas [LK95] divide requirements into *market-oriented and customer-oriented requirements*. Products that are developed on the basis of market-oriented requirements usually have no specific customer for whom the system is to be built. There is instead a specific group of customers who are the potential buyers of the product, which could be a word processor or a spreadsheet. Customer-oriented requirements are those where a customer has a specific problem that has to be solved. This is yet another distinction between software, system and product requirements.

In [BI96], Boehm and In use the term *quality attribute requirements* to describe software quality attributes relating to the software architecture and software process.

3.4.1   Types of Requirements

To be able to manage or trace requirements, we need a way of classifying them. The larger and more intricate the system, the more types of requirements occur. A requirement type is simply a class of requirements. Identifying types of requirements helps firstly to organize large numbers of requirements into meaningful and manageable parts or groups, and secondly to structure and design the system.

Types can be decomposed into other types. Business rules and statements can be types of high-level requirements from which user needs, features and product requirements can be derived. From use cases and other forms of modelling, other types of requirements like design requirements can be decomposed into software or system requirements, which represent the analysis and design models.

In the literature, two main requirements are distinguished: functional and nonfunctional requirements. These are described in the next two subsections. Functional requirements reflect the functionality of the system to be build, whereas nonfunctional requirements are much harder to qualify, classify and to handle in the software process. Therefore nonfunctional requirements are described in a more detailed way.

3.4.2   Functional Requirements

Functional requirements capture the intended behaviour of the system. This behaviour may be expressed in the form of service, tasks or functions the system is required to perform. Functional requirements reflect the question of what the software should do. According to [oEE90], functional requirements define the functions that software must perform. They describe operations the software or one of its components performs on its inputs to produce outputs.

Functional requirements can be described from the point of the data, or from that of the functionality or behaviour of the system that is to be built.

- From the point of view of the data:
  Here, we look at the data structures data structure in the application domain. The concepts are entities , relationships, attributes and data values that describe the properties of an entity. Data represents a static view (e.g. Entity-Relationship Modelling) [Che76].

- From the point of view of functionality:
  Here, we look at the software from the point of view of input/output activities, e.g. activities transforming a set of inputs into set of outputs. Data flow diagrams are examples [Ros77, RS77].

- From the point of view of behaviour:
  Here, the system is looked at from the states of the software and transitions between states and events which trigger the state transaction. Examples of such behavioural models are statecharts [Har87].

Object-oriented modelling integrates all three: data, functionality and dynamic modelling. In Fusion, the models that reflect these views are: Class Model, which models the data view, Life Cycle Model, which describes the functionality; and Operation Model, which describes the dynamical view.

3.4.3 Nonfunctional Requirements

During the requirements engineering process – and throughout the software development process – the non-functional requirements must be given the same or even more attention than the functional requirements.

It is the nature of science to pursue a functional model of reality, and the nature of art always to lie beyond that pursuit. Although the boundary between the two may change with time and the development of technology, science and art remain complementary.

Embedded systems or information systems, like all complex engineering products, exhibit essential features from both sides of the boundary. Those on the formalized scientific side are called functional requirements; those on the other are called nonfunctional requirements. To suppose that all requirements could ever become functional would be as naive as to suppose that science could one day embrace art.

The purpose of this brief outline is to explain where the boundary between functional and nonfunctional requirements now lies, and to indicate the variety of concerns that are spread across it. We begin by setting the historical context.

In the beginning, there was code. When programmers worked with machine code, there were no explicit functional requirements. With the advent of high-level languages and large programming projects, software engineering was born, making contracts between customers and suppliers necessary. Input/output behaviour provided the first functional requirements [Dav93], all else remaining nonfunctional. As formal methodologies, focussing on the I/O model of computation were developed, time and space efficiency constituted the most pressing nonfunctional requirements (although little-used formalizations have since been developed to place them in the functional domain (e.g. [Jac95])).

As PCs became popular, their software demanded user-friendly interfaces and requirements documents began to contain substantial nonfunctional requirements, most of which have remained nonfunctional to this day. While ergonometric concerns could conceivably be formalized, those of design resemble art so closely that it is unlikely they ever will be.

Fifteen years ago, security was regarded as a major difficulty, largely because it was nonfunctional. Since then, several security properties have been formalized and thus converted into functional requirements. On the other hand, some features of security, like those pertaining strongly to human-computer interaction, seem destined to remain on the nonfunctional side. Must a machine be locked to the desk, for example, to prevent the physical theft of software? Security and safety are typical areas which currently straddle the boundary between functional and nonfunctional requirements.

The same holds for user interfaces in a more general sense. Certain properties are amenable to formal specification and so can be expected to be formalized as functional requirements. Colour and location on the screen, for example, can be described formally (by wavelength and Cartesian coordinates, respectively). But features pertaining more to design and based on taste and intuition appear destined to remain nonfunctional.

The requirements considered so far pertain to the product. There is an equally important range of requirements pertaining to the process. Organizational or management requirements, for example, are often a consequence of organizational policies and procedures, and hence are concerned more with the process than the product. Other examples include implementation requirements like target programming language, design method and delivery requirements (e.g. delivery deadlines and consequent financial penalties); they are usually formalized. Such requirements, which may be generated by either the customer or the developer, are just as relevant to the success of the project as product-based requirements.

Interoperability requirements determine how the system is to interact with other systems; legal requirements force the system to operate within the law; ethical requirements ensure that the system conforms to accepted ethical standards; and more generally, social and ethical requirements deal with the acceptability of the system to its users and the general public. All these features cover requirements arising from factors external to the system itself and its development process.

The view outlined here has, of course, evolved gradually. Alan Davis talks instead about behavourial requirements and nonbehavourial requirements [Dav93]. Behavourial requirements define what the system does; they specify the inputs (stimuli) to the system, the output (responses) from it, and the behavourial relationship between them. Nonbehavourial requirements are those describing the required overall attributes of a system, including portability, reliability, efficiency, human engineering, testability, understandability and modifiability.

Michael Jackson [ZJ97, Jac95] has proposed an alternative way to look at context. His focus is more on the problem than on the solution, as is reflected in common current practice. Requirements are about purposes, and the purpose of a machine (or software) is found outside the machine itself, namely in the problem context. He distinguishes between properties that are purely environmental, called indicative properties, and those that represent the interface between the environment (domain) and the machine, called optative properties. He takes a much broader view of the problem context than anyone else. In [Jac00], he states: "The distinction between functional and nonfunctional requirements is a reasonable distinction to make, and is often useful. But there's a serious risk that it becomes an excuse for ignoring important requirements and concerns." Most requirements that are nonfunctional are so only in the sense that they have not yet been analyzed. If you allow requirements like these to be relegated to the nonfunctional category, you risk missing a large part of your problem.

Various classifications for nonfunctional requirements or quality requirements have been proposed. Earlier efforts were made by Barry Boehm and Ho [BI96]. Nowadays the community is concentrating on nonfunctional requirements because of the possibility of managing software components through them. Also, the practice of including nonfunctional specifications in the contract and monitoring them strictly can be expected to become more popular in the future [Szy98].

Nonfunctional requirements are particulary affected by changes in hardware technology. The development time for large systems may be several years, while hardware will continue to improve throughout the lifetime of the system and even during its gestation. Nonfunctional requirements may thus have to be modified while the system is still in use.

3.5   The Requirements Engineering Process

Requirements engineering aims to define the requirements of the system under construction.

3.5.1   Elicitation

Requirements elicitation is the process of discovering the requirements for a system by communication with the customers, system users, analysts and others who have a stake in the system development. It requires application domain and organizational knowledge as well as specific problem knowledge [SS97]. Elicitation is about gathering information. The question is what kind of information should be gathered and how to gather it. Traditional techniques for requirements elicitations include interviews, questionnaires, observation and the study of business documents [GL93].

- Interviews are a key fact-finding and informations-gathering technique. They are simple and cost effective. Most interviews are conducted with customers or with domain experts. Whether an interview is successful depends on many factors, the most important being the interviewer's communication and interpersonal skills.

- Questionnaires are an effective way of getting information from the customer. They are normally used in combination with interviews. Questionnaires should be designed for ease of question answering. There are several forms including multiple-choice rating and ranking questions. Combining interviews and questionnaires can be a successful technique for elicitation.

- Observation can be either passive or active. There are situations in which a customer is unable to describe a business or technical process. In this case observation is an effective way of fact finding. Observation should be done in combination with interviews and questionnaires or with one of the two.

- A more modern elicitation technique involves the use of the software prototypes Joint Application Development (JAD) and Rapid Application Development (RAD). They help us to obtain a better understanding of the requirements by visualizing the Graphical User Interface (GUI) of the system at a very early stage using mock-ups, for example.

3.5.2   Analysis and Negotiation

Requirements elicited from customers may overlap or conflict. Some requirements may be ambiguous, unrealistic or inconsistent. Others may remain undiscovered.

For these reasons, analysis is necessary. The objective of requirements analysis and negotiation is to establish an agreed set of requirements which are complete and consistent. Requirements analysis and negotiation are concerned with high-level statements of requirements elicited by the stakeholders. It is an expensive and time-consuming process. These requirements are then developed in more detail as specifications or models. Developing such models usually reveals further contradictions and incompleteness in the requirements. In this case, it is necessary to repeat the elicitation and negotiation phase to discuss changes in requirements.

With the initial set of requirements, it is possible to define the boundaries of the system being built. This involves determining which of the requirements are system requirements, which are for the operational processes associated with the system, and which requirements should be outside the scope of the system, though belonging to its environment.

3.5.2.1 Some Analysis Techniques

Domain Analysis

This technique can be used to expand the scope of the requirements elicitation, to identify and plan for anticipated changes, to determine fundamental commonalities, and to support the creation of robust architectures. Feature modelling facilitates the identification and analysis of the product line's commonality and variability and provides a natural vehicle for requirements specification. Stakeholder-view modelling supports the completeness of the requirements elicitation.

Viewpoint Modelling

This technique can be used to support the prioritized modelling of the significant stakeholder requirements for the system being built. Viewpoint modelling is based on the recognition that a system must satisfy the needs and expectations of the various stakeholders, all of whom have their own perspectives (views) of the system. Each stakeholder view can be modelled separately as a set of system requirements. These models are core assets that support the identification of conflicts and can be used to determine trade-offs between the needs of the stakeholders [KS97, SS97].

3.6 Traceability of Requirements

Requirements traceability can be used to ensure that the design and implementation of a system satisfy the requirements for that system. Requirements traceability traces the requirements backwards to their source (e.g. a stakeholder) and forwards to the resulting system development work products (e.g. a system class model or a component). In addition to helping with the elicitation and verification of requirements, requirements traceability is critical in determining the potential impact of proposed changes in a system [RSE95, Som01].

The main risk associated with requirements engineering is failure to capture the right requirements over the life time of the product. Documenting the wrong or inappropriate requirements, failing to keep the requirements up to date or to document the requirements at all puts the architect and the component developers at a grave disadvantage. They will be unable to produce systems that satisfy the customer and fulfil market expectations. Inappropriate requirements can be the result of:

- Failure to distinguish between system requirements and domain requirements: these different kinds of requirements have different audiences. The developers need to know the requirements they must build to.

- Insufficient generality in the requirements leads to a design that is too rigid to deal with changes in the product.

- Overly general requirements lead to excessive effort in producing both the software and specific products (which must turn that generality into a specific instantiation).

- Failure to account for qualities other than behaviour: software requirements in general should capture requirements for quality attributes such as performance, reliability, security, and the like. These are nonfunctional requirements.

One way to minimize the risk of failing to capture the right requirements for the product is to classify, test, verify, version and trace requirements.

3.6.1 Tracing

The development and use of requirements-tracing techniques originated in the early 1970s to influence the completeness , consistency and traceability of the system's requirements.

Requirements traceability is defined as the ability to describe and follow the life of a requirement, in both a forwards and backwards direction (i.e. from its origins, through its development and specification, to its subsequent deployment and through periods of ongoing refinement and iteration in any of these phases) [GF97]. It can be achieved by using one or more of the following techniques:

- Cross-referencing: this involves embedding phrases like "see Section x" throughout the project documentation (e.g. the tagging, numbering or indexing of requirements, and specialized tables or matrices that track the cross-references).

- Specialized templates and integration or transformation documents. These are used to store links between documents created in different phases of development.

- Restructuring: the documentation is restructured in terms of an underlying network or graph to keep track of requirements changes (e.g. assumption-based truth-maintenance networks, chaining mechanisms, constraint networks and propagation) [GF95, GF97].

Chapter 4

Formal Methods

Even today, formal methods are considered too complicated in certain software engineering circles. This view is taken not only by people from industry but also by computer science students who are being trained as software engineers. The first ideas and concepts for formal methods were published fifty-five years ago.

Initially, researchers focused on ways of verifying that a program or a system satisfied its specification (or that two programs were equivalent). Over the last fifty-five years, it has become clear that formal verification is only practical for very small programs. From this point on, verification methods supported the development of programs. For larger programs or systems, it is necessary to utilize a notation of composition [Smi00, Mor90] in order to handle the task. A program can only be judged to be correct with respect to some independent specification of what it should achieve, e.g. a requirements specification or formal specification. Testing alone cannot ensure the correctness of even relatively straightforward programs. If bugs are to be avoided, some technique other than testing must be used to establish that software satisfies its specifications.

This chapter begins with a historical introduction, showing where the most influential work in the history of formal methods came from. It was done by people like von Neumann, Turing, Floyd, McCarthy, Naur and Hoare. Other important work could be considered, but this would go beyond the scope of this chapter. The next section deals with formal methods in general. It introduces two formal state-based specification and their techniques that are of major interest for this book: Z and its extension, Object-Z. Object-Z is a formal state-based method for object-oriented systems. Fusion/UML is an object-oriented development method. System operations, described in the Operation Model in the analysis phase of Fusion/UML, are expressed in a quasi formal way based on Object-Z.

4.1   A Historical Look at Formal Specification

As early as 1947, Goldstine and von Neumann wrote a paper in which they explained how assertion boxes can be used to record that a series of operation boxes (flow charts) have a particular effect. They pointed out that the task of coding is nontrivial.

> Our problem is, then, to find a simple, step by step method, by which these difficulties can be overcome. Since coding is not a static process of translating but rather a technique of providing a dynamic background to control the automatic evolution of a meaning, it has to be viewed as a logical problem and one that represents a new branch of formal logics.

To master this, their basic design approach was to plan from flowcharts. They introduced the concept of "assertions" in combinations of flow diagrams:

> Next we consider the changes, actually limitations, of the domains of variables of one or more bound variables, individually or in their interrelationships.

In 1949, Turing introduced the idea of a Turing machine as a thought experience to prove formal systems. He saw the need to address the issues of program correctness and termination. He prepared the ground for the subsequent trailblazing work of McCarthy, Floyd, Naur, Hoare and Dijkstra, to name just a few of the many who worked on this topic over the next forty years.

At the Western Joint Computer Conference in 1961, John McCarthy defined the issue as the Mathematical Theory of Computation. The development of this relationship demands a concern for both applications and mathematical algorithms. It plays an important role in formally describing the semantics of programming languages, and indeed for all languages, including UML. Language semantics cannot be considered separately from program verification. McCarthy focused on reasoning about recursive functions rather than on imperative programs and languages, which was the focus of research at this time, e.g. Algol 60. His goal was to prove that given procedures solve given problems: "instead of debugging the program, one should prove that it meets its specifications and its proof should be checked by a computer program."

Floyd and Naur were working independently on the same idea of program verification at about the same time. Floyd's work was more recognized than Naur's because Floyd presented his idea with a sounder mathematical foundation. But both greatly influenced research on program verification.

Floyd's (1967) method is based on annotating a flowchart. The generality of using first-order predicate calculus for assertions and the explicit role of loop invariants are his key contributions. Floyd gives precise verification conditions which ensure that the assertion corresponds to the statement in the flowchart. Floyd was the first to offer formal rules for checking verification conditions. Operational semantics originated in Floyd's work.

Naur's Snapshots were written as comments in the text of Algol60 programs and are clear statements about relationships between variables. His approach was a less mathematical one, which is probably why it was less recognized by the community.

Hoare (1969) not only linked the ideas of van Wijngaarden and Floyd but also gave program verification a big boost by turning a theoretical idea into an applicable technique in the direction of formal methods. It may be said that Hoare realized that a program is already a formal model, and that in principle it is possible to derive all properties of a program using a logical calculus. The behaviour of a program depends on the environment in which the program is embedded. A program always communicates with its environment, otherwise it would be of little use.

Hoare looked at sequential programs. A sequential program communicates with its environment when it reads input parameters, and after termination when it outputs its result. The environment is therefore given by the precondition, given by the requirements of the program through its parameters.

In the following sections, we look at formal methods, more specifically those which use a state-based approach.

4.2 Formal State-based Methods

Formal methods are an approach to software engineering that is based on the application of mathematics, e.g. set theory, predicate logic, algebra, etc. Some formal methods such as Z, VDM and Larch focus on specifying the behaviour of sequential systems. States are formulated in terms of mathematical structures like sets, relations and functions. State transitions are described as pre- and post-conditions. Other formal methods such as CSP, Statecharts and Temporal Logic focus on specifying the behaviour of concurrent systems. States are specified from simple domains like integers to sequences, trees or partial orders of events.

All these methods use a mathematical concept of abstraction and composition. This underlying approach is to describe the system or specify it in mathematical terms, the output being the formal specification.

The process of specification involves writing down requirements precisely. The main benefit of doing so is to acquire a deeper understanding of the system being specified. Through this process, developers uncover design flaws, inconsistencies, ambiguities and incompleteness. The specification can be a useful platform for communication between customer and designer, designer and implementer.

In the next two sections, two key formal state-based methods are explained: Z and Object-Z. The first section deals with Z, the second with Object-Z. Fusion/UML has much in common with Z and its extension Object-Z. The operation schema is one of the artefacts of the analysis task used in specifying the system change of state triggered by the system operation. The change in the system state is described in the style of Z and Object-Z, respectively.

4.2.1   Z

The formal specification Z [Spi92] was developed by the Programming Research Group at Oxford. A Z specification normally defines a number of state and operation schemata.

The Z notation is based on set theory and mathematical logic. Set theory includes standard set operations, set comprehension, Cartesian products and power sets. The mathematical logic is a first-order predicate calculus. This is the mathematical language of Z.

Z is a strongly typed language. A type is an expression of a structured term, which is either a given set name or a compound type built from simpler types using one of a small number of type constructors. Each expression in a Z specification has a unique type and each variable has a type that can be deduced from its declaration. Each specification starts with objects that have no internal structure of interest. These atomic objects are members of the basic types or given sets of the specification. The basic type of Z is $\mathbb{Z}$, whereas integer is only a member of the basic type $\mathbb{Z}$, defined in the mathematical toolkit of Z.

More complex objects are defined through basic types, composite types and type constructors. Composite types are set types, Cartesian product types and schema types. The type construct can be applied repeatedly to obtain increasingly complex types with an increasingly complex structure.

The other aspect of Z is that the mathematical can be structured. Objects and their properties can be expressed in terms of schemata: declaration and constraints. The schema language is used to describe the changes in state of the system and how such changes may alter. It can also describe the system properties, e.g. invariants. There are different kinds of schemata: the state schema, which describes the global state of the system and the system invariants; the init schema, which defines the initial state of the system and operation schemata. The schema calculus enables us to specify total operations.

An important part of the Z method is the standard library, called *toolkit*. In the library, a set of basic operators of the set algebra, like relations, functions, natural numbers and finiteness, sequence and bag, are defined.

4.2.2 Object-Z

Object-Z is an object-oriented extension of the formal specification language Z. It makes use of many of Z's features, including schema notation for defining operations. [Smi00] writes: "In fact, Object-Z is a conservative extension of Z in the sense, that all Z's syntax and its associated semantics are also part of Object-Z. Therefore, any Z specification is also an Object-Z specification." An object-oriented enhancement of Z offers support for encapsulation, inheritance and polymorphism, the paradigm of object-orientation. As already mentioned in the previous section, schemata and the schema calculus are very powerful techniques for structuring and defining its own operations. One weakness of the original Z is that there is no mechanism for splitting or modularizing large specification into parts.

Object-orientation offers a powerful mechanism for splitting the specification into a number of interacting classes and objects. A specification in Object-Z consists of a set of classes. Each class defines an interface, a class state and an initialization, together with a number of perations that change the state.

There are different ways of structuring classes in specifications. One way is *inheritance*. A class may inherit another class. This allows complex classes and specifications to be built from simpler components in an iterative fashion. This mechanism is used in schema inclusion at operation level (schema calculus)

The other way is instantiation. A class is a template for objects of that class. It enables classes to reference objects of other classes as state variables. Polymorphism can be applied by instantiations by allowing objects of a subclass to be substituted where an object of a superclass was expected.

A complete Object-Z specification includes a number of interacting class definitions. Apart from classes that define the behaviour of the specified system, global type definitions, abbreviations and declarations can be introduced in the same way as in Z.

A general class definition has the following form[Smi00]:

```
  ┌─ ClassName[genericparameters] ─────────────────────────────
  │  visibility list
  │  inherited classes
  │  local type definitions
  │  local constant definitions
  │  state schema
  │  initial state schema
  │  operation schema
  └────────────────────────────────────────────────────────────
```

- visibility list explicitly lists those features that are visible to the objects of the environment. Features can be classes, constants, state variables, initial state schema and operations. If no visibility list is given, then all features of that class are visible to its environment.

- inherited classes denote those classes that are inherited by the defining class.

- type and constant definitions are type definitions and axiomatic definitions. Because of the use of reference semantics for objects (variables declared to be of a class type are considered to be actually (variable) pointers to objects of the class), it is often the case that instances of supplier classes are defined via pointer constants in the constant definition part of an Object-Z class. In this case, the pointer constant serves as the name for the modifiable object that is pointed to.

- state schema is an anonymous Z schema that declares the attributes and state space of the class. These attributes may be of a class type.

- initial state schema defines a set of possible initial values for the attributes of the class.

- operation schemata use the schema notation of Z to define state transitions (denoted by dashed and undashed variables). However, a $\Delta - list$ is a list of state variables that may be changed by the operation, and only these variables. This means that all state variables that do not appear in the $\Delta - list$ remain unchanged.

$\quad$ _stack[T]_ _____

$\qquad$ $max : \mathbb{N}$

$\qquad$ _____

$\qquad$ $max \leq 100$

$\qquad$ $items : seq\,T$

$\qquad$ _____

$\qquad$ $\#items \leq max$

$\qquad$ _INIT_ _____

$\qquad$ $items = \langle\,\rangle$

$\qquad$ _push_ _____

$\qquad$ $\Delta(items)$

$\qquad$ $item? : T$

$\qquad$ _____

$\qquad$ $\#items < max$

$\qquad$ $items' = \langle item?\rangle \frown items$

$\qquad$ _pop_ _____

$\qquad$ $\Delta(items)$

$\qquad$ $item! : T$

$\qquad$ _____

$\qquad$ $\#items \neq \langle\,\rangle$

$\qquad$ $items = \langle item!\rangle \frown items'$

The class defines a constant max of type $\mathbb{N}$. Max will never exceed 100. The state schema has one state variable *items*, a sequence of type T and a class invariant which ensures that the number of elements of the sequence will never be more than *max*. The initial schema denotes that the initial stack has no elements. Operation *push* inserts the input *item?* as the first element of the existing sequence of items, but only if the number of elements of the sequence do not exceed the maximum size of the sequence. The value of the state variable *items*, denoted by ', after the operation has been evaluated, is denoted by the right side of the equation. The operation *pop* outputs the value of *item!*, defined as the head of sequence items, and reduces the sequence items to their original value, but only if the stack is not empty.

When a class is applied, the actual parameter $\mathbb{N}$ replaces the generic types, e.g. *stack*[$\mathbb{N}$].

In addition to replacing the generic parameter by actual types, attributes and variables can be renamed as well. Renaming encompasses the whole class with simultaneous substitution indicated by the list pairs: *item* to *nat*, *item?* to *nat?* and *item!* to *nat!*:

$stack[\mathbb{N}][nat/item, nat?/item?, nat!/item!]$

Renaming is mostly used in inheritance to allow attributes and variables to be renamed in order to avoid name clashes.

4.2.2.1   Object-Z Schema Calculus

The Object-Z schema calculus is like the calculus in Z. Using the calculus, complex operations can be built systematically in an iterative manner. Object-Z offers seven operation operators: conjunction $\wedge$, choice $[\!]$, sequential composition $\overset{\circ}{,}$, the parallel operator $\|$, enrichment $\bullet$ and hiding $\backslash@!$.

When using the binary operators to combine two operations into a new operation, the usual rules of type compatibility are used to merge two declarations into one. In addition, the $\Delta - lists$ of the operations are merged so that the new operation can change any variables that either of its two operations could have changed.

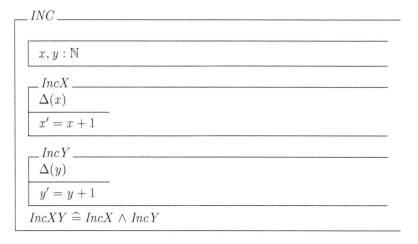

The operation IncXY has the same effect as the operations $IncX$ and $IncY$ performing at the same time. $IncXY$ increments both x and y simultaneously.

Object-Z has three special operators, the *Distributed Operators* $\wedge$, $[\!]$ and $\overset{\circ}{,}$. They are based on the binary operators $\wedge$, $[\!]$ and $\overset{\circ}{,}$. Distributed operators are very useful when specifying operators that involve an arbitrary number of objects (cf. Appendix A).

Part II

Fusion/UML So Far

Fusion [Cea94] is an object-oriented development method for producing software. The method's notation is based on the original Fusion Method, extended and modified by [BK00] using UML [JBR98]. The method supports analysis, design and implementation in the software development process. The software developer is guided throughout the process, from analysis right through to implementation. This involves developing several different models of the software being built, which are partially transformed from one model to the next and checked for consistency.

In the next two chapters, we describe the Fusion/UML method, the main subject of the book. The extensions made to this method are explained in part III. The next two chapters describe the analysis and design processes, their models and model elements and the consistency between the models.

In line with the common software development life cycle, FusionUML distinguishes between analysis, design and implementation. In this book, we focus exclusively on analysis and design.

46

Introduction to the Fusion/UML Process

The goal of analysis from the user's point of view is to understand and describe the external behaviour consistencies. Contradictions should be detected and eliminated. Implementation is not considered in this phase.

Analysis

Analysis models are described as follows:

- Classes of objects that cover the whole application context (Class Model)

- Requirement-relevant relationships between these classes

- Operations by which the user can communicate with the system (system operation) and the reaction of the system to system operation system operation (system events). These steps could lead to a significant extension of the former Class Model.

- Acceptable sequential order of these system operation and the reaction of the system (system events) to them.

At this point in development, FusionUML does not look at system functions on the level of class routines (methods) as other object-oriented development methods do.

Design

The aim of design is to develop an abstract implementation concept for the system operations identified in the analysis phase. These operations are transformed in the runtime behaviour into interacting objects. To obtain the interface definitions of classes, the reference structure of the modelled associations and the inheritance structure have to be fixed.

Implementation

The programmer's task is to translate the design models into executable code in a programming language. The FusionUML method offers guidance on how to go about this.

- Inheritance, referencing and class attributes are implemented in classes of the chosen programming language.

- Object interactions become class methods.

- The accepted sequence of operations is realized by the runtime system of the chosen programming language.

At the end of each modelling phase, FusionUML offers a consistency test which guarantees that none of the models is in conflict with another.

In addition to all the models for the different phases, FusionUML has one model – the Data Dictionary – which collects all model elements throughout the development process.

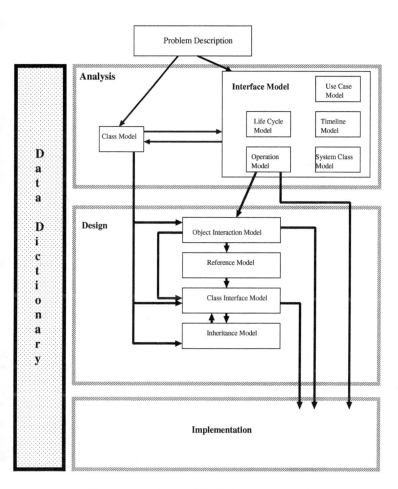

Figure 4.1: Fusion/UMl Analysis and Design Models

50

Chapter 5

Analysis

5.1 The Process and its Models

Analysis must be done stepwise, each step being connected to a characteristic model. The goal is to find a comprehensive model of the problem domain, and within this problem domain to find a solution henceforth referred to as the *System*. Through systematic elicitation of user interaction, the boundary between the *System* and its *Environment* is fixed. Analysis therefore results in a static class model (application domain) and a dynamic interface model (a specification of the system's external behaviour).

Step 1: Objects and concepts within the problem domain are described in a Class Model using the object-oriented Entity-Relationship Model for modelling elements. It is a static-structure module.

Step 2: Communication on a high level of abstraction between the role of the user and the system is specified using so-called UML use case diagrams. Here, the function groups of the system are defined.

Steps 1 and 2 should not be executed in strict sequence because their views are complementary and do not overlap.

Step 3: The use case is refined by means of scenarios taking the form of timeline diagrams. Timeline diagrams are notated as *sequence diagrams* in the UML style. The modelling elements are system operations and system events. The Use Case Model and the Timeline Model form the system interface.

Step 4: As a result of fixed user communication, the boundary between the environment and the system inside the (static) Class Model can be specified. The outcome is the System Class Model. This step implies the previous steps (1, 2 and 3).

Step 5: All identified system operations are included in a global system behaviour.

This is specified in a Life Cycle Model using regular expressions. All system operations and sytem events must be identified in this model. Steps 2 and 3 are prerequisites for this step.

Step 6: The semantics of every single system operation are specified in the most detailed manner possible using elements of predicate logic. This is specified in a so-called operation schema. All of these form the Operation Model. This step – the most important in the whole of the analysis phase – requires at least the Timeline Model, the System Class Model and the Life Cycle Model.

Use Case Model, Timeline Model, Life Cycle Model and Operation Model form the Interface Model.

The Data Dictionary is the central reference glossary in Fusion. Every identifier that is a modelling element, e.g. classes, associations, attributes, roles, system operations, system events, etc., is entered in the Data Dictionary, which includes the definition of each item. This ensures the semantic consistency of all models – at least informally.

5.1.1   Analysis Models and their Notation

Existing documents of this kind are often ambiguous and probably inconsistent. The aim of analysis is to work out a description of the system's behaviour that is clear, complete and free of contradiction.

A couple of models are created during analysis reflecting what the system should do rather than what the system will do. This kind of approach can be explained by the perspective user. Analysis thus has to deal with the system domain and model the system according to the domain. The analysis phase produces two models, which focus on and describe different aspects of the system:

- The *Class Model* defines the static structure of the domain (environment) by describing relationships between classes, objects (subjects) and facts that reflect the real world.

- The *Interface Model* defines input/output communication between the environment and the system.

5.1.2   Data Dictionary

The Data Dictionary is used throughout the Fusion process. It consists of term definitions (expressions and names) and concepts. The system is specified when the definitions of all elements of all models are complete. The Data Dictionary plays a key role in consistency and completeness checking of all models.

Name	Kind	Description	Source
name of the entries	class, system operation, attribute, etc.	informal description	all models in which the name appears

Figure 5.1: Structure of the Data Dictionary

If necessary, new columns for specific kinds can be introduced. There is no required format for the Data Dictionary, but the following requirements for entries should hold:

- Definitions should have an unambiguous name so that they can be found easily.

- Aliases should be avoided.

- Items should not occur more than once.

- No superfluous information should be entered in the Data Dictionary (e.g. in the column description).

- The Data Dictionary should refer to those documents in which the explained items have been used.

During the analysis phase, all items of the Class Model and its Interface Model should be gathered in the Data Dictionary. They include classes, associations, attributes, system operations, system events, actors and expressions.

Example:

In the following example, some terms from the analysis are defined in the Data Dictionary.

Name	Kind	Description	Source
Bank	class	A bank consists of multiple accounts	Class Model, System Class Model, etc.
open_account	system operation	A customer opens a new account at the bank	Timeline Model
account.number	attribute	account of the bank customer	Class Model
transaction	regular expression	A transaction is either through withdrawal or selecting a bank statement.	Life Cycle Model

5.1.3   The Class Model

The representation of the Class Model is based on the extended *Entity-Relationship* Model [Che76] and the UML (Unified Modeling Language) [JBR98].

5.1.3.1   Objects and Classes

An **object** is an abstraction of real "things", concepts or complex issues (facts) that exist in the context of solving problems. They have a clearly defined meaning. Each object must be clearly distinguishable from another. It has its own identity, which is unchangeable.

Values can be associated with each object. These are elements of a fixed set of types (e.g. integers, real numbers but also elements, which can themselves be objects). According to Fusion, the strict typing with associated values is insignificant. Later on in the design – and of course in the implementation phase – they play an important role.

Attributes of an object must be fully declared in every model in which this object holds. However, they can be screened out. UML uses the term *suppressed*, meaning that one does not have to write them down in a diagram according to the requested abstraction even though they are present. Several (nonidentical) objects may have the same attributes and attribute values.

Other dynamic characteristics of the objects are modelled during design. The graphical representation is extended (cf. Chapter 6).

The associated values of an object are identified by an unequivocal identifier, as so-called attributes of the object. Attribute values are handled and changed by their identifiers (which is why incorrect modelling usually causes the association of the object identification to be taken as an attribute). Attribute identifiers and the number of attributes cannot be changed.

A class is an abstraction of a number of homogeneous objects. A predicate belongs to each class. It defines the criteria for the class relationship of the objects. This kind of implicit predicate constitutes the homogeneous behaviour, and thus the class itself. Moreover, the similarity (of the identity) and dissimilarity are definable for any two given objects of a class (with identical behaviour).

A class always has a name , and attributes can be defined for classes. This means that all objects (or instances) of the same class must have the same attributes (but not the same attribute values). The homogeneity (same behaviour or semantics, respectively) of the objects of a class is based on statements of the values of the same attributes and on statements of their relationships to other objects.

According to Fusion, a class is graphically represented in the analysis as a rectangle with a horizontal separation. The modelling element for the classes of UML is always planned for at least two horizontal separations. For methodological reasons, only one separation is allowed here because methods of a class should not be modelled in the Fusion analysis. The upper part of the rectangle contains the class name, which always begins with an upper-case letter. The lower part contains a list of attribute names. Classes correspond to entities in the *Entity-Relationship Model*.

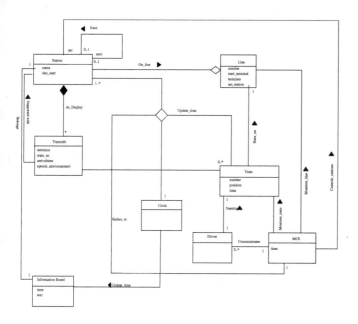

Figure 5.2: An example of a Class Model: Daisy-Soft

??

5.1.4 Associations and Links

In the *real* world, objects relate to each other, for example, *Holds* is a relation between professors and their lectures. Such a relation is called a link and can be mathematically modelled as an ordered tuple of objects. On the class level, such relations are seen mathematically as relations, i.e. a set of tuples of objects. In set theory, a relation is a partial set of the Cartesian product of the participating classes (set). The same set can also appear in the product. The most frequent case is the binary relation, which consists only of ordered pairs of objects from two classes.

All object-oriented analysis and design methods model relations through associations between classes. The meaning of the modelling element association transcends the mathematical term *relation*. Thus, all stages of the involved classes are specially screened as to whether there are one or more tuples of objects that exist or do not exist as components (totality). This property means that the specification of the association always implies that objects cannot be in a relation to other objects, except where otherwise specified. As described later on, association has further properties which also extend the narrow mathematical term of *relation*. A binary association is graphically represented as a continuous line connecting two classes. Note that an association can also connect a class with itself.

A ternary or higher-order association (a rare case) is represented as a rhombus connected by lines with all the involved class symbols.

An association can have a name, which is placed in the middle of the connecting line or, in the case of a ternary association, close to the rhombus (cf. Fig. 2.7.). The name is a string of signs beginning with an upper-case letter, to which a filled-in triangle is added to show the reading direction. An association does not have to be named. It may also consist only of the classes and the association line. The filled-in triangle is part of the name and does not imply a specific direction of an association. Associations are static relations that cannot represent an operational link between objects, like message passing or navigation. For this reason, they have no direction with respect to the mentioned concepts. Associations between classes correspond to the relationships in the *Entity-Relationship Model*.

5.1.5   Roles

Further properties can be specified for associations. Some properties are connected with a role, which corresponds to the arity of the involved objects in the mathematical relation. Graphically, the roles of an association are connected with the ends of the unbroken line when they reach the involved classes. The ends of the associations can have names. These names indicate the roles of the classes in the association end. The names of the roles are in lower-case letters.

5.1.5.1   Multiplicity

An important specification of a role fixes the area of the allowed cardinality of class objects that are involved in an association. Expressions of multiplicity do not have to be declared. Multiplicity indicates the exact or the maximum number of objects that can be in a relation with an object at the other end (or other ends) of the association. The following forms are possible:

- A number, e.g. 10 (exactly 10 objects can be related to all but one object of the other classes and all objects together relate to any of the objects of the other classes (totality)).

- An area, e.g. 1..4 (a minimum of one and a maximum of 4 objects relate to each but one object of the other classes and all objects relate to any of the objects of the other classes (totality)). An area, e.g. 0..1 (either no object relates to the objects of the other classes or exactly one object relates to each but one object of the other classes and all objects together relate to any of the objects of the other classes (no totality)).

- The asterisk-symbol * stands for a non negative whole number (either no object relates to objects of the other classes or any number of objects relates to all but one object of the other classes and all of the objects relate to any of the objects of the other classes (no totality). A asterisk symbol can also be used as an upper limit of an area. The assigned value of the * must not contradict the specification of the lower limit. 1..* means that * can never have the value 0.

- A list of areas separated by commas, e.g. 1..3, 5..7, 13..* (any number of objects except 4, 8, 9, 10, 12 relate to all but one object of the other classes and all objects relate to any of the objects of the other classes).

- If a multiplicity is not explicitly given, this means*

The figure shows a simple Class Model with multiplicity and association between the classes students, professors, lecture and instantiation (faculty). This example expresses the following facts:

- Each institute is headed by one professor at the most.

- There is an institute that is not headed by a professor.

- There are professors that do not head an institute.

- Professors can give any number of courses or no courses at all.

- A course can be given by two professors at the most.

- There are courses that are not given by a professor.

- Every student has to enrol for a minimum of four and a maximum of six courses.

- There are at least three students enrolled in each course.

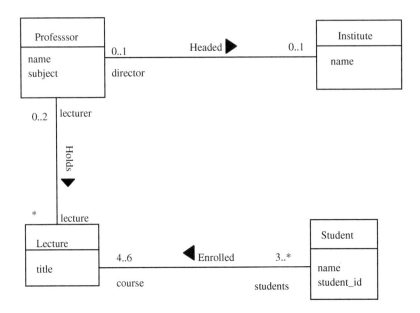

Figure 5.3: Multiplicity

The multiplicity of an association can be specified in Z. This is illustrated by two associations *Headed* and *Enrolled*.

Headed ▶: *Professor* ↔ *Institute*
$\forall\, i : Institute \bullet \#\{p : Professor \mid (p, i) \in Headed ▶\} \leq 1$
$\forall\, p : Professor \bullet \#\{i : Institute \mid (p, i) \in Headed ▶\} \leq 1$

◀ *Enrolled* : *Courses* ↔ *Student*
$\forall\, s : Student \bullet \#\{c : Course) \mid (c, s) \in ◀ Enrolled\} \in 4..6$
$\forall\, cCourse \bullet \#\{s : Student \mid (c, s) \in ◀ Enrolled\} \geq 3$

5.1.5.2   Association Classes

Like objects and classes an association can also have attributes. This makes sense, if properties cannot be associated to any of the classes involved with the association. If, for example, one considers the association *writes* between the classes *student* and *test*, one can assign the attribute *mark*, which indicates the mark given to a *student* in a particular test. The attribute *mark* cannot be an attribute of the class *student* (a student usually writes more than one test) or an attribute of the class *test*, because a test is written by several students.

The rectangle, which is connected with the association line by a dotted line, has the same name as the association (optional) and has attributes. It is analogously chosen as a normal class symbol, but it only becomes significant when combined with the association line.

The arity indicates the number of classes of a particular association. So far, we have examined only binary associations, but tenary or unary associations are possible. By way of an example, let us look at the class *room* in the association *writes*, which indicates the room where the test was written.

5.1.5.3 Aggregation and Composition

A very important and often used property of an association role is *aggregation*. The specification of *aggregation*, graphically represented by a small empty rhombus, can only occur at one role of an association at the most and distinguishes this role as an aggregate. This design is used as a means for structuring the Class Model at points where one wishes to express a close relationship of single objects (components) to an aggregated object. Thus, associations with an aggregation specification are also considered as *part of a whole* or *part of relations*, which the aggregation's role unsymmetrically distinguishes as a whole and the rest of the involved objects as parts. If an association provided with the aggregation specification has no further attributes, the association name is often omitted because the part of a relation describes the semantics quite sufficiently. In the general form of aggregation, it is possible for a component to be part of more than one aggregate (shared aggregation).

The special case of component objects only being connected in a part-whole relation to exactly one aggregated object (container) is termed composition (unshared aggregation). Furthermore, composition components can no longer exist as their aggregates are also called compositions. The multiplicity of the composition role is 1. There are several possible representations for composition:

- Normally, the composition role of the aggregate is represented by a filled-in rhombus at the end of the particular association that connects the aggregate with its components. If all of these associations are undeclared or equally declared, the association lines can be wholly or partly combined from the aggregate to the particular component. In all other cases, separated association lines should be used because of the unequivocal coordination.

- The close relationship between the components and their aggregate becomes more obvious by using the nesting of components together with the relations between them in the rectangle, which indicates the composition. Generally, the association lines in this case are drawn from the edge of the aggregate inwards to the components. The lines can also be omitted. The

decoration of the redundant associations (role names, multiplicity, etc.) can
be transferred: in the class symbol, the role name is written as an attribute
name and the class name as a type indicator. The multiplicity is written
in the upper right-hand corner.

- The modelling of the components as regular attributes of the composition
  goes a step further. But in this case all possible relations between the
  components within the other representations have to be suppressed. In this
  representation, the information is lost. If a coarser model is required, this
  representation should be chosen.

5.1.5.4   Types

A type is the specification of a behaviour of elements by declaring type names,
typed attributes, functions and their semantics, expressed in a strictly formal
language, e.g. by axioms as equations or in a semiformal notation like UML. All
elements corresponding to a type specification define the carrier set of the type.

In the object-oriented world, a type is implemented by a class. One can say
that the instantiations of this implementation class are of the implemented type
or have the implemented type. Moreover, this implementation class can be an
abstract class in the sense of the programmed language, e.g. its state cannot
be created as objects. Implementation classes can also be concrete classes depending on the programming language, or further steps are needed to concretize
their realization. The above-used term implementation should not be understood
merely as a translation into a computer language.

We now turn to instantiations of implementation classes, regardless of whether
such instantiations are abstract (not applicable to the computer) or concrete
(applicable to the computer as objects).

Fig 5.6 shows that the algebraically specified types Stack and Queue are implemented by the same implementation class Stack_or_Queue. An instantiation
of Stack_or_Queue therefore has either the type Stack or the type Queue. One
reason for implementing several types using the very same implementation class
is to transfer both type structures using the same implementation type. In our
case, Stack[G] and Queue[G] can also be represented by the (also algebraically
specifiable) type Sequence[G]. Stack and queue only differ from each other in that
one can add (push) or remove (pop and top) elements to/from the stack at the
same end of the sequence (LIFO, Last In First Out), whereas one can add (put)
elements to the queue at one end of the sequence and remove them at the other
end of the sequence (remove, item)(LIFO, Last In First Out).

G is therefore an optional unspecified type, which is used as a formal type parameter of stack that can be renewed by an optional type. This principle is called

types
    Stack[G]

functions

push:	Stack[G] × G	→	Stack[G]
pop:	Stack[G]	↠	Stack[G]
top:	Stack[G]	↠	G
emptys:	Stack[G]	→	Boolean
news:	Stack[G]		

axioms
    $\forall x : G, s : Stack[G]$

top (push(s,x))	=	x
pop (push(s,x))	=	s
emptys (news)	=	**true**
$\neg$ emptys (push (s,x))	=	**true**

preconditon

pre (pop(s))	=	$\neg$ emptys(s)
pre (top(s))	=	$\neg$ emptys(s)

Figure 5.4: Algebraic specification of the type Stack

types
    Queue[G]

functions

put:	Queue[G] x G	→	Queue[G]
remove:	Queue[G]	↠	Queue[G]
item:	Queue[G]	↠	G
emptyq:	Queue[G]	→	Boolean
newq:	Queue[G]		

axioms
    $\forall x : G, q : Queue[G]$

item (put(q,x))	=	**if** emptyq(q) **then** x **else** item(q) **fi**
remove (put(q,x))	=	**if** emptyq(q) **then** q **else** put(remove(q),x) **fi**
emptyq (newq)	=	**true**
$\neg$ emptyq (put(q,x))	=	**true**

preconditon

pre (remove(q))	=	$\neg$ emptyq(q)
pre (item(q))	=	$\neg$ emptyq(q)

Figure 5.5: Algebraic specification of type Queue

genericity, type specification using unbound formal parameters (not to be confused with generalization (cf. Section 5.1.5.5). Stack[G] $\rightarrow$ Stack[G] is a total function in which each element of Stack[G] is possible as the domain. Stack[G] $\twoheadrightarrow$ Stack[G] is a partial function in which not all of the elements of Stack[G] are possible as the domain of the function. In our case, the empty Stack/empty Queue are not domains, a fact that is additionally indicated by the preconditions.

In UML, implementation classes can be denoted by using the stereotype <<Implementation class>> in front of the class name. According to UML, stereotypes are additionally introduced modelling elements, denoted by <<>>, each of which shows great similarity to the already defined modelling elements, which most likely differ in terms of their limitations.   Thus, an <<Implementation class>> behaves like a class of which no real objects need exist in the execution model. If one can be certain that there are no such limitations, the stereotype <<Implementation class>> corresponds to the modelling element class. Our implementation class Stack_or_Queue has an attribute element of the type Sequence [G].

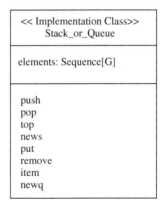

Figure 5.6: Implementation class: Stack_or_Queue

Relations can exist between types. For example, a type (supertype) can specify a partial behaviour of another type (subtype). This relation can thus be mapped onto the corresponding implementation class of supertype and subtype as a generalization/specialization relation (Gen/Spec relation). Fusion generally assumes that an implementation class comforms to only one type specification, which is implemented by this class. To this extent, type and implementation class can be identified by their use. Thus, in the analysis of Fusion there is no notational distinction between type and class (i.e. types cannot be presented yet; UML has extended presentations). Classes can therefore always be interpreted as types. Additionally, type and class names can be used to specify attributes versus classes as elements of a type. Attributes are either stated by an elementary type (i.e. by Standard Definition Boolean, Integer, String, etc.) or by a class type. In Fusion, it is not necessary to explicitly type an attribute during analysis.

5.1.5.5   Generalization and Specialization

The Gen/Spec relation for classes already introduced in the previous section is graphically represented by a triangle connecting the supertype (represented by its implementation class) with the subtype (represented by its implementation class) or each subtype separately with the supertype. The figure also shows that each undergraduate studies element and each advanced studies element has an attribute title besides the specified attributes. One can say that objects of the subtypes inherit the attribute title. The semantics of the Gen/Spec relation states that each undergraduate studies object behaves like a lecture object. The Gen/Spec relation is often termed (or rather misinterpreted) as an *is-a relation* (with respect to the super type). It is often mistaken as a set inclusion and should rather be called a *behaves-like* relation. The specialization of a super type by a subtype can be restricted to additional specifications (in this case, constraints) of the *Gen/Spec relation.*

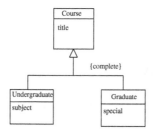

Figure 5.7: Gen/Spec Relation

Permitted restrictions are:

- complete
  The modelling process is finished; no additional subtypes can be modelled at a later stage of the software development process.

- incomplete
  The modelling process is unfinished because additional subtypes could be added at a later stage of the software development process.

The constraint specification is annotated beside the Gen/Spec triangle in curled brackets.

Notes:

1. The Gen/Spec relation is a relation between types or classes. It is not an association that is instantiated by links between objects.

2. A subtype (subclass) can be in a Gen/Spec relation to several supertypes (superclasses). Thus, each object of the subtype inherits properties of several superclasses. This process is called multiple generalization. The opposite process – a class becoming a subclass of various super classes – is called multiple specialization.

5.1.6   Use Case Model

The starting point for all further modelling is the Use Case Model. Other object-oriented methods also use this kind of argument. *Use Case Analysis* thus often precedes the real analysis as a specific step in the modelling process.

In the Use Case Model, the system-external roles (actors) and their functional behaviour (communication) towards the system are identified. Conversely, the attempt is made to identify, define and, if necessary, structure the mutual relations of the functional groups (use cases) of the system with regard to their individual roles. Often the Use Case Model is used to structure the behaviour of the system via processes, a process not necessarily being only one operation sequence. A use case is defined as a number of action sequences. Sequences are actions that follow one another in time. They will later be precisely defined as scenarios in the Timeline Model. Action sequences of the same use case can – but need not – relate to each other. However, a use case is not process modelling in the classical sense. The criterion for the definition of use cases is a conceptual behaviour scope towards functional scenarios.

On the one hand, use cases are defined as being behaviourally independent of one another. On the other hand, their behaviour is related via three possible kinds of relations. The Gen/Spec relation between two use cases defines a common dynamic behaviour of their super use case. Specialized use cases concretize (realize) the common behaviour by making several distinctions without a conceptual extension of this common behaviour towards the actors.

Use Cases only describe it exactly, i.e.

The Gen/Spec relation between use cases is closely analogous to the Class Model. An <<include>> relation between use case A and B (A<<include>>B) expresses that the behaviour of A cannot be modelled without the behaviour of B; A presupposes B. B never appears by itself, i.e. there is no direct relation to an

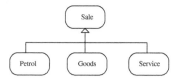

Figure 5.8: Use case – Gen/Spec relation

actor. This dependence is denoted by a dashed arrow. It is used wherever a behaviour A is significantly extended towards a behaviour B. An <<extend>> relation between use case B and use case A (B<<extend>>A) is a dependence that specifies the extension of the behaviour of A only in particularly well-defined cases.

The modelling presupposes the declaration of the cases by extension points in A. In general, the entire semantics of A partly presupposes the behaviour of B.

Use case modelling focuses on the communication behaviour of the system (or parts of it) with the environment. This modelling does not explicitly relate to the Class Model of the system on this level of abstraction. Class modelling and use case modelling are global views of the system that are independent of each other. Since actors correspond to the stakeholders in requirements analysis, the use case reflects different domain areas and requirements.

The Use Case Model as a global diagram takes the following form:

A use case is represented as an ellipse and has a name. Actors can communicate with one or more use cases, indicated by a straight line (no communication direction). All use cases are located within the system represented by a rectangle with an (optional) name. Use cases as a limited behaviour of the system can communicate with an actor. The retrieval of use cases is an abstraction step that derives from a real scenario and combines with it to form a united behaviour. Conversely, every use case can be instantiated in the course of additional refinements by different scenarios. In exactly the same way, it is abstracted from concrete human or other instantiations (persons, hardware or software components, etc.) by introducing the actors symbol. It is important to note that actor instantiations are located outside the system.

5.1.7 Timeline Model

Scenarios of use cases are specified in detail by timeline diagram. They serve as a reminder that the definition of use cases is the accumulation of a set of action sequences. All possible action sequences of each use case of the Use Case Model are systematically identified and specified. An action sequence is expressed

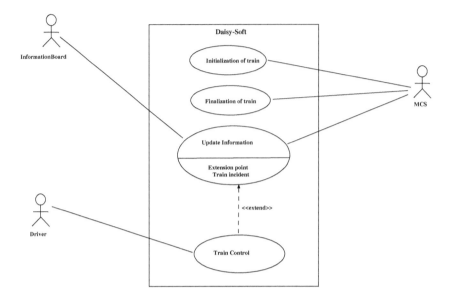

Figure 5.9: Daisy Soft: Use Case Model

by a scenario. In FusionUML, each scenario is realized by a timeline diagram. Timeline diagrams are so called because they model communication events within a certain time frame.

Active communication events that derive from actors are called system operations (or input events). System reactions that are directed towards the actor are called (output events) system events. The communicative interplay between actor and system is within time, or to be more precise: an exact or relative moment is not modelled but is rather a temporal before/after sequence. Timeline diagrams can be seen as reduced sequence diagrams of UML, here without a time scale.

A timeline diagram consists of vertical lifelines, which are associated with any involved actor or the system in the scenario. The availability of any actual instantiation in time is indicated by the lifelines (the time running vertically from top to bottom). Arrowed lines from the actor instantiation to the system represent system operations, which are declared with their name and additional details, e.g. arguments or parameters.

Arguments of system operations and system events are concrete values in the case of scenarios and must be suitably declared. Arguments of system operations are declared values from the application context (whose structuring cannot be presumed to be object-oriented). Arguments of system events, on the other hand, are values of object attributes because of the object-oriented structure of the system. Since no concrete object instantiations have been specified so far, in the case of the arguments one can follow the same rules as for the actor or the system instantiation: anonymous class instantiation is used on the argument's position:

- If object attribute values are used, the Class Model (and the Data Dictionary) must contain these attributes in the matching classes.

- All actors as classes must relate in an association relation to at least one other class belonging to the system (consistency rule between Timeline Model and System Class Model).

In the same way, system events are represented by continuous arrowed lines from the system to the actors instantiation. Here too, as in the system operations, arguments can be given to the names. Actor instantiations and the system are objects (starting with actor classes and the system class, respectively) according to the syntax and the semantics of UM. They are represented as rectangles in which the instantiation is anonymously denoted by:

:actorname
:systemname

This kind of notation, as in UML, must be briefly explained: actorname and systemname are class stereotypes (classifiers) in UML. They correspond to abstractions of instantiations with the same behaviour (in the case of classes with the classtype; in the case of the actor, with the communication semantics). Instantiation is denoted in UML by underlining the abstract element from which the instantiation is formed. :actorname is an anonymous instantiation of this abstraction.

5.1.8 System Class Model

The System Class Model is a partial model of the Class Model . It is graphically denoted as the interior of an area of a Class Model, enclosed by dotted lines (cf. A.4). It models the system with all the system-internal classes as part of an entire system environment .

Provided that actors, system operations and system events are already modelled, it is relatively easy to implement classes and associations of the Class Model belonging to the system (corresponding to use cases) or located outside the system (corresponding to actors). System operations might require additional extension of the System Class Model. The two main reasons for such an extension are:

- Partners in the communication between actor and system. At this point, one should already think about each system operation and which object

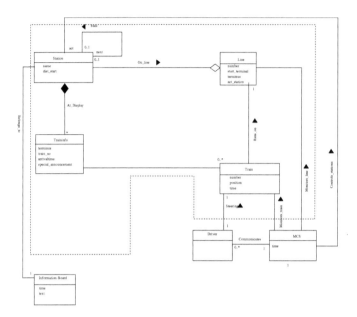

Figure 5.10: Example of a System Class Model

in the interior of the system can be the communication partner of the
actor and initiate the system operation (input event). If such a matching
partner is not available, a corresponding internal object must be modelled
and the System Class Model System Class Model possibly extended by a
new class (in one of the next models the communication partners are called
controllerss).

- Actor attributes. The actor can correspond not only by sending an event
  but also by means of additionally typed communications attributes (later
  called parameters of the system operation). Since system operations as
  parameters are components of the system, the parameter types can be basic
  types. Otherwise, they must also be specified by class definition in the
  system system if they do not yet exist in the Class Model (to differentiate
  parameters from system objects, cf. 5.1.10).

The System Class Model is a well-formed Class Model. Thus, the association
that exists between the classes inside and outside the System Class Model is
automatically outside the System Class Model and no longer relevant to the
system. In general, the limits of the System Class Model should be tightly drawn:

- All classes needed for modelling the behaviour of an actor that do not model
  the communication with the system are outside the System Class Model.

- All classes that are not directly necessary for realizing the semantics of the System Class Model are deleted as redundant from the System Class Model.

5.1.9 Life Cycle Model

The timeline diagram describes an action sequence, which represents a communication scenario of one or more actors with the system. The Life Cycle Model, on the other hand, represents a globally running scenario of the system. Actors do not explicitly appear in this model, but all system operations and system events without explicit parameters do. These are the two basic modelling elements. The expressive strength of this model also rests on additional modelling elements for representing repetitive runs, parallelism, alternatives and composition. In this way, the Life Cycle Model describes the whole application process, which in general can be rather complex. Therefore, one obviously needs to introduce structuring elements (so-called abbreviation expressions) to master the complexity of the overall process. We have discussed this analogously in the section 5.1.3.

An abbreviation expression is also the specification of a partial process, whereas here, unlike to the timeline diagram, this partial process is realized as part of the whole. Ignoring this context is one of the most frequent mistakes made in designing the Life Cycle Model. For example, if partial processes were introduced by abbreviation expressions on the highest abstraction level:

$P = A \mid B \mid C$

A, **B** and **C** define alternative paths. These run from a starting point to the finishing point of the system and can never be combined.

An example of a Life Cycle Model:

Lifecycle DAISY-Soft	=	(Initialize_train_journey; train_journey*; Finalize_train_journey ∥Update_information)*
Initialize_train_journey	=	establish_train; #infos_established
Train_journey	=	Train_leaves_station; (Arrives_at_station | Train_has_stopped)
Train_leaves_station	=	leave_station; #info_updated
Arrives_at_station	=	arrive_at_station; #info_updated
Train_has_stopped	=	train_stopped; #info_updated;continue_journey; #info_updated; arrive_at_station; #info_updated

Finalize_train_journey   =   remove_train;#train_is_removed

Update_information   =   deliver_new_infos; #infos_delivered

5.1.10   Operation Model

So far, we have defined the static environment of the problem using the Class Model. The first step towards solving the problem involves modelling the dynamic behaviour of the problem with respect to its environment by means of use cases and timeline diagrams. From this dynamic view of the problem solution, a modification and limitation of the static Class Model to the System Class Model is derived. This leads us to the next step in modelling. Naturally, this step is an extension of the dynamic view, but now mapped to the statistical object structures of the system, which are provided entirely by the System Class Model.

The Operation Model consists of the specifications of all changes of the system state, each of which is caused by one system operation. The system state is therefore defined as the state of all system objects in the form of attribute assignments and the relations between the objects in the form of links. A change in the system's state is defined as a change in the state of the system objects and/or a change in the relations (links) between them. In addition, all reactions of the system are specified by the operation schema in the form of events that are triggered by the system operation. This kind of specification of a system operation is called an operation schema.

Operation schemata exclusively define the effect of changes of state in the form of predicates. There are no means of expression for controlling them or temporal runs that show how and when the effect emerges. In the operation schemata, initialization procedures of the overall system are not taken into account because they are, at this point in the analysis, not relevant to the dynamics of the system. A system operation can cause the following changes of state:

- Existing objects change their state by changing their attribute values.

- Objects as instantiations of classes are created or deleted.

- Links as instantiations of associations are created or deleted between objects.

- Attribute values of links can change themselves.

This means:

- The system is regarded as consisting of instantiations of classes (objects) and instantiations of associations (links).

- Objects and links are either persistent or transient; they either belong to the topology of the system or are movable data of a dynamic process.

In an operation schema, the change of state is described by the declaration of pre- and postconditions. In this way, it is generally referred to as the precondition in the form of extensive case differentations.

With regard to the Operation Model, the following statements have to be made in general. A system operation is run by concrete (i.e. created and therefore identifiable) objects. It can create them as an effect ({new}), delete them ({delete}) or in the course of the execution create and later delete them ({transient}). Such effects can be annotated in the operation schema but not specified. The objects and attributes that can be accessed by a system operation are called variables. Attributes are values that are needed for the specification of the system operation and are not associated with an existing object or attribute. They are always of a certain type, which does not need to be declared because it always results from the context. Arguments and variables together form the state of the operation. The postcondition therefore specifies a change of state.

The general form of an operation schema for system operation $sysop_i$ is:

Operation	=	$sysop_i$
Description	=	...
Input	=	$i_1 : I_1, \ldots, i_n : I_n$
Reads	=	$r_1 : R_1$ **with** $P_{R_1}, \ldots, r_k : R_k$ **with** P_{R_k}
Changes	=	$c_1 : C_1$ **with** $P_{C_1}, \ldots, c_l : C_l$ **with** P_{C_l}
Sends	=	$: A_1 : \{s_1\}, \ldots, : A_m : \{s_m\}$
Pre	=	P_{pre}
Post	=	P_{post}

The parts of an operation schema are:

- The name of the system operation starting with the keyword Operation.

- The verbal description starting with the keyword Description.

- The part starting with the keyword *Input* contains the arguments of the system operation. Arguments are communication attributes that are declared by the actor as additional information for the system operation and therefore delivered to the system by the environment. The types of the argument values (if they are specified at all) are either basic types, of which the specification is generally predefined (like number, text, etc.), or class types, which are declared in the System Class Model (i.e. within the limits of the system).

- The part starting with the keyword *Reads* contains all objects, links and attributes (of objects and links) that belong to the definition of the precondition of the operation. The operation can reference their values without changing them.

- The part starting with the keyword *Changes* contains all objects, links and attributes that can possibly change the operation. A special case is the identification of an object of the implementation class of its type by declaring a selection condition: Type_name with condition. In the list of the objects and links, the specific manner of the status change can – but must not – be declared by creating (*new*), deleting (*delete*) or the declaration of a lifetime during the system operation (*transient*) by declaring the keyword behind the object or link identifier.

- The events triggered as a reaction of the system to this operation are listed under the keyword. *Sends*, the receiver being declared as the name of the actor. System events are the only modelling elements by means of which the information flow (output value) can be modelled from the system to the actor. System events are atomic in their purest form.

- The predicate of the operation is placed after the keyword *Pre*. According to the following principle of design (design by contract), the user environment of the system operation must meet the precondition if the postcondition is valid. Conversely, if the precondition is not valid the postcondition does not need to be true: If a party to a contract violates the contract conditions, the other party need not fulfil the contract conditions, i.e. if the environment violates the contract (meets the precondition), the operation need not fulfil the contract either. The aim of the FusionUML method for specifying system operations is to enhance robustness by already modelling all possible reactions of the system in the timeline diagrams, which must therefore be shown as effects in the postcondition of the operation schemata. This normally makes the system operation applicable without any further precondition. In other words, the precondition is the weakest possible one and is therefore true and default. In this case, the pre-part can be missing. Generally, the pragmatic rule is applicable because the formulation of the pre-part should be as independent as possible from different special application contexts. Only those conditions should be acknowledged that are always valid and relate to the modelled system status. Preconditions also contain cases, which result from the mathematical design, to formulate the postcondition.

- The part starting with the keyword *Post* specifies the effect of the system operation by change of state and system events. This can only be made possible by a predicate, in which values of the precondition are related to values of the postconditon status. Normally, the predicate consists of case differentiations in the form of implications, which are combined by conjunction. The syntax of the predicates is based on the formal specification languages Z and Object-Z. Thus, attribute values of the postcondition states are marked with ' after their name. All possible postcondition states of the operation are given by value reservation of object or link attributes. The post-predicate can be evaluated as true.

This example of an operation schema is taken from the Case Study DAISY-Soft:

Operation	=	leave_station
Rational	=	When the train leaves the station all arrival times of all train infos of all subsequent stations will be updated.
Input	=	$train, line$
Reads	=	$act : Station$ **with** $first(t.position) = act$ $On\_line, Succ$ $l : Line$ **with** $l.number = line$
Changes	=	$t : Train$ **with** $t.train\_no = train,$ $At\_display, Traininfo$
Sends	=	$: Driver : \{info\_updated\}$
Pre	=	**true**
Post	=	$t.position' = (act, Succ(act))$ **is_sent** $\{info\_updated\}\ \wedge$ $(\forall s : Station \mid (s,l) \in On\_line$ $s.dist\_act - act.dist\_start > 0 \wedge (s, act) \notin Succ \bullet$ $info.train\_no' = train \wedge$ $\quad (\exists i : Traininfo \mid (i, start) \in At\_display' \wedge$ $\quad\quad i.train\_no = train \bullet$ $\quad\quad\quad i.arrivaltime' = s.dist - act.dist\_start + sojourn))$ $(\exists s : Station \mid (s,l) \in On\_line \wedge (s, act) \in Succ \bullet$ $\quad (\exists i : Traininfo \mid (i, l.start_t erminal) \in At\_display' \wedge$ $\quad\quad i.train\_no = train \bullet$ $\quad\quad\quad i.arrivaltime' = s.dist - act.dist\_start))$

An operation schema in FusionUML is an arranged sequence of tagged values.

Their tags are denoted keywords and their values can be expressed by semiformal specification languages. Regarding the kinds of diagrams used in UML, an operation schema is an additional specification of the already modelled system operation in the timeline diagram. Such additional element properties can be attached to a modelling element by commentary (free text), limitations (formal or semiformal languages) or marked values (tagged values). In this case, the whole operation schema is attached to any system operation of the timeline diagram as a sequence of tagged values. In the UML notation, this is done by putting the operation schema in curled brackets.

5.2   Consistency Check

In this section, we do not look in detail at the consistency check between model elements of a model and between models themselves. We refer to a degree thesis [Böh02] supervised by the Software Engineering research group at the TU Berlin.

The two aspects of analysis model checking are consistency and completeness.

- Completeness
  A model is complete when it captures a meaningful abstraction in the domain. Completeness is a concept which is quite hard to fulfil in the software development process. At what time an iterative analysis process should end, is a decision that must be made by someone involved in this process, e.g. the analyst. There is only one way to check completeness and that is against requirements.

- Consistency
  Models are consistent when they do not contradict each other. This means that the modelling elements that are used in a model and that occur again in another model must retain the same meaning and may, at most, be semantically extended. It also means that the use of specific modelling elements in a (previous) model enforces the use of submodels or modelling elements in another (subsequent) model. Ideally, a uniform, consistent semantic model should be sought for all models. One approach is to introduce a Data Dictionary valid for all models, in which all modelled elements must occur and be checked for consistency.

  They should not contradict each other either implicitly or explicitly. Explicit inconsistency is shown in the Data Dictionary. Implicit inconsistency in a model is hard to find unless a semantical model of this model exists. In Fusion, the semantics of the analysis models are defined but informally (cf. Appendix B).

Examples of simple consistency checks are:

- For each use case at least one timeline diagram must exist. This is an example of enforcing the use of the modelling element of a timeline diagram, which comes from a definition of a use case of the previous Use Case Model.

- All classes, associations and attributes used in the Operation Model must appear in the System Class Model. All predicates must be defined in the Data Dictionary. However, this does not rule out the addition of further attributes in the Operation Model, which must, of course, be consistent with the already existing ones.

- The boundary of the System Class Model is consistent with that of the Use Case Model. All actors defined in the Use Case Model must appear in the System Class Model and Timeline Model.

- All system operations and their system events in the Timeline Model must appear in the Life Cycle Model.

- Each system operation in the Life Cycle Model has a corresponding operation schema.

- All identifiers in all models have entries in the Data Dictionary.

- The output of events of the Life Cycle Model and Operation Model must be consistent. The schema for a system operation must generate the output events (system events) that are modelled in the timeline diagram.

Chapter 6

Design

In the design phase we are looking at the models built during the phase and design of a system that has the behaviour described in these models.

6.1   The Process and its Models

As pointed out in the previous chapter, the aim of the object-oriented design process is to develop an abstract implementation concept for the system that has been specified by the analysis. During the analysis the system's functionality is considered and specified almost exclusively from the global point of view of the user. In the operation model, too, which represents the most detailed specification of the analysis, effects are represented exclusively by changes of state on the already identified objects. There are no statements made in which dynamic runs are responsible for these change of states. The task design is to model these dynamics completely.

The advantage of all object-oriented methods (including Fusion/UML) is that they can be used on the basis of already existing static analysis models, which are enriched with additional information without invalidating the analysis models.

The aim of Fusion design is to give an abstract description of class interfaces. It is also desirable to establish the reference structure between objects as far as possible.

Throughout the system development process all models developed so far are valid and necessary for the overall understanding of the problem domain. Each model deliberately emphasizes certain aspects and suppresses others.

During system evolution, then, all models must be continously developed and their mutual consistency ensured.

The design is limited by semantics of the specified partial functionality, which cannot be modelled without the semantics of a concrete programming language. Only during implementation is an (abstract or concrete) algorithm design possible, which can lead to a execution model of the system. The first step in design is the formulation of one object interaction graph for each system operation or operation schema . For this purpose, the information of the corresponding operation schema is used. An object interaction graph is a dynamic model that models the communication between the objects of the operation schema by named message passing. This method enables interfaces to be partly fixed between classes of the objects used in the operation schema.

In the second step, all client-server relations between the classes of the system are derived from the object interaction graph. The direction of the message passing is therefore decisive. The reference of a client to its server(s) is also termed the visibility of the server. In most cases, the reference of a relation between client and server can be expressed by a client attribute in the class description. There are other cases in which the client-server relation is short lived. Therefore it can only be decided during implementation whether or not the corresponding reference is included in the class interface.

In such cases, the principle of the postponed decision does not require the creation of a premature implementation binding through modelling as client class attribute. The referencing model established in this second step is realized in UML by annotated class diagrams. Constraints or tagged values are used for this purpose. In the third step, one can now establish a class interface description. It remains incomplete:

- Only the complete implementation provide a complete interface description.

- The class relations can be extended by inheritance properties.

The latter always applies if common features can be factored out of the interfaces of two or more classes. Besides, one may have to decide if the already modelled Gen/Spec relations of the analysis can be transformed into inheritance relations between class interfaces . In the fourth step, this can be achieved by extension of the Class Interface description. The central Data Dictionary has to be updated during design , too, by the inclusion of new modelling elements or annotations etc..

6.1.1   Object Interaction Model

This first model of the Fusion design is the key specification of the structure and behaviour of all system operations. The model therefore consists of individual object interaction graphs. In other words, for each of the defined system operations there is exactly one corresponding object interaction graph (i.e. there is a one-to-one relationship between system operations and object interaction graphs).

The structure of a system operation has already been prepared in the operation schemata of the analysis. The objects of the system operation that have been determined in the Reads and Changes parts can be written down and complemented by the links derived from the System Class Model (they follow from of the associations modelled!) there. This structural specification of an object interaction graph is called collaboration, following UML. It determines precisely all the objects a system operation needs to achieve its effects.

The next step is the modelling of the *behaviour* of the operation, which can only be executed by annotation on the collaboration. The behaviour is expressed by specifying as completely as possible (but in an implementation-dependent manner) the decentral flow of control, which is triggered by an external actor using the system operation.

In Fusion, as in UML, the basic elements of the control flow are called *Messages*, which are sent from one object to another. They are directed and can only flow along the links modelled in the collaboration. A message is represented as an arrow between the source and target object, parallel to the existing link. The arrow is labelled with the exact specification of the message. This specification contains as its most important element the name of the procedure that calls the source object and which is later implemented in the target object. The message flow can be structured using classical structuring elements of the flow of control such as sequence, iteration and hierarchy. The flow of control that matches a collaboration is called interaction, following UML. The structure of the collaboration guarantees that it contains exactly those objects that are needed to specify the process that is triggered by the call of the system operation. For this purpose, the call of the system operation is regarded as a message between an actor and an exclusive object of the collaboration. This exclusive object is called a *controller*, unlike all the other objects of the collaboration are called *collaborators*.

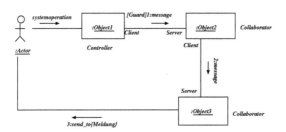

Figure 6.1: Object interaction graph

Once the controller and the arguments of a system operation call have been determined, the process triggered by this call has to be further specified. In Fusion, it is assumed that each process consists only of sequences of messages that are triggered one after another. More precisely: the effect, namely the termination of the call of a procedure of an previous message triggers the following message. Such a sequence is called message flow. It is terminated by the termination of its last procedure call. The corresponding message specifications are numbered in ascending order by natural numbers. This number precedes the message name and is separated from it by ":"

Each procedure call can trigger a new message flow, whose termination is the precondition for its own termination. Such a sub-message flow is labelled in the same way with sequence numbers, but it is preceded by the sequence number of the triggering message in decimal notation.

The transmission of a message can depend on a condition i.e. the interpretation of the condition as true/false is the precondition for the procedure call. If the condition is interpreted as false, the specified message is considered to be terminated and the next message in the message flow is evaluated. The repeated evaluation of a message expression can also be specified.

In this case, the corresponding procedure call, together with all subsequences, is iterated until a termination condition is fullfilled. The objects that were newly created or deleted by the system operation or are transient and were annotated in the operation schema by new etc., can be marked after the object name with new etc. The corresponding procedure call for creating a new object is **create**.

6.1.2   The Reference Model

When establishing the object interaction graph , it has so far been assumed that all objects can, in principle, send each other messages. The property by which a client object can send a message to a server object is called referencing of the server by the client. The unlimited referencing is, however, limited by the fact that it requires links.

All the objects of the Object Interaction Model are checked to determine the role they play in the collaborations: clients or servers or both. A graph is now established for each client. Its basic structure consists of the client itself, the corresponding servers and the existing links between them. For this modelling, no elements are used that specify the behaviour (e.g. message flows). This model can therefore be implemented again on the abstract level of classes and associations. As further annotations of this graph, four additional attributes play a role (modelled by tagged values or constraints):

   1. The reference lifetime, keyword **reference**; the attribute specifies whether

a reference of the client to its server exists only during the procedure call or for a shorter time; in this case the attribute is dynamic – or longer, for example during the whole lifetime of the client – in this case the attribute is permanent. The annotation is attached to the client role of the existing association.

2. Mutability, keyword **mutability**. The attribute specifies whether the referencing remains unchanged during the whole lifetime of the client or whether it changes. The latter is the case if server objects are newly generated. The annotation is attached to the association between client and server.

3. The visibility of the server, keyword **visibility**. The attribute specifies whether only one (exclusive) or more (shared) clients have access to the server. The annotation is attached to the server class.

4. If a client object can refer to more than one server object of the same class, this can be expressed explicitly by a specification at the server role of the association by the keyword **col**.

Figure 6.2: Example of a reference graph

6.1.3 Class Interface Model

The class interface brings together the properties of the system determined during design by providing a linear textual description for each class of the system: the referencing interface of the class. It contains information about the names and types of class attributes and about the names and parameterization of procedures. In addition, during specializations between classes and modelled generalizations analysis will be taken into account or rejected and new generalizations may be introduced. The following elements and properties are considered:

- All classes, which appear in the collaborations of the design or in the System Class Model .

- All attributes of a class

- All methods of a class and its parameter

- The type of the attributes either data type or type of the attribute-implementati
  class in the case of a permanent reference.

- Composition relations between aggregates and constituting components.
  These relations are called bindings. They have the value *bound*, if composed
  or *unbound* if not composed. Default is unbound.

- Mutability of a reference, default is var.

- The use of a referenced server class viewed from the client class (visibility),
  it conforms with the visibility of the server. Default is shared.

The following are not modelled in the class interface:

- The reference lifetime dynamic, because this depends on the actual way a
  procedure is implemented.

- All properties of the message flow; they can only be taken into account by
  concrete implementation of the algorithms in a programming language.

It is therefore clear that not only the class interface but also all models of the
design and the analysis phases form the basis for the implementation.

```
class Bank\\
attribute name:Text\\
attribute account: col exclusive account\\
methode open_account(customer:customername)\\
method ...\\
method ...\\
endclass Bank\\
```

6.1.4 Inheritance Graph

A first version of the class interfaces, initially lacks Gen/Spec relations. They
can be added according to two different criteria:

1. Gen/Spec relations already existing in the Class Model are examined to
   determine whether it makes sense both attributes and methods of the super
   class to be inherited.

2. A comparison of the class interfaces may indicate that not only common attributes of classes but also common methods can be "factored out". There must not necessarily be a meaningful super type/sub type relation in terms of the problem. Introducing additional Inheritance is generally a software engineering decision for optimizing the system implementation.

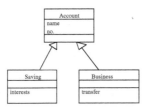

Figure 6.3: Example of an Inheritance graph

Newly acquired inheritance structures are specified as behaves-like relations between the newly acquired super types (class) and sub types (class).

```
class Saving behaves_like Account\\
attribute ...\\
attribute ...\\
method charge_interests()\\
..\\
endclass Saving\\


class Giro behaves_like Account\\
attribute ...\\
attribute ...\\
method credit_transfere()\\
method withdraw_standing order()\\
...\\
endclass Giro\\
```

6.2 Consistency Check

Consistency of the design models are checked against models of the analysis phase. We will only present the most important ones. For a more detailled consistency check we refer to a master thesis [Böh02] done at TU Berlin.

- *Object Interaction Model:* Each class of the System Class Model should be represented in at least one object interaction graph.
  It should be checked that the functional effect of each object interaction graph satisfies the specification of the system operation given in the Operation Model. This an example for the need of a unified semantical model for operation scheme and object interaction graph (cf. Section 8.2).

- *Reference Model*: For each association on the System Class Model there has to be a path of visibility for the correspondent class of the reference graph.
  Exclusive objects must not be referenced by more than one class.

Class Interface Model: There must be checks to ensure that all methods and parameters from the Object Interaction Model, all data attributes from the System Class Model and all class attributes from the reference model are recorded.

Inheritance graph: Check whether superclass and subclass(es) are entered in the Class Interface Description.

Part III

The Extensions of Fusion/UML

In the next two chapters, the changes to the Fusion/UML process and its new modelling elements and the consistency checks are explained.

88

Chapter 7

Enhancement – Determining Requirements

To develop software is to build a system by describing it. On a general level, the relationship between a software system and its environment is clear. The system is introduced to have an effect. Part of the environment will affect the system and be affected by its application domain. Here, the customer can judge whether the development has fulfilled its intended purpose. The distinction between the application domain and the system is the key to the much-cited distinction between WHAT AND HOW [Dav93]. WHAT the system does is to be found in the application domain, while the HOW is the system itself. The problem is in the application domain, and the system is the solution. Development methods claim to offer an analysis of the problem, when in fact they merely offer an outline of a solution, leaving the problem unexplored and unexplained. The requirements are located in the application domain; that is where the problem is and nowhere else.

Michael Jackson writes in [Jac95]: "A problem is characterized less by the nature of the machine you will build than by the structure and the properties of the application domain and your customer's requirements in the application domain. Any software development needs many descriptions. The complexity of most software problems does not allow one to think about the whole problem at once. You need to find a way of separating the problem in parts, called separation of concerns. Which means concentrating on a partial problem and leave the rest for later. The outcome of such separation are partial descriptions. The art of separation is to find the right abstraction and partitioning. Descriptions are the external visible medium of thought. If you understand how descriptions work, and how one description differs from another, you can use this understanding to improve your techniques for thinking about problems."

In the previous chapter, the method with its process, models, the consistency between model elements and between models and the heuristics were described in detail, except for those parts that extend this method. In this chapter a detailed description of the requirements determination is given. The process of determination is illustrated by an example that has already been introduced to describe the method in the previous chapter.

The extraction of requirements both from the domain and for the system are explained in the next section. The classification of requirements and the types of requirements are explained. This is followed by a discussion of how to formalize requirements formally where possible. In the last section of this chapter, the determination process and the impact on those models of $Fusion_B$, the Use Case Model and the Domain Class Model are described. Furthermore, the linking of requirements and tracing is explained.

7.1   The Process of Determining Requirements

$Fusion_B$ does not begin with the first activity of the requirements engineering process, requirements elicitation (cf. Section 3) but expects a problem description in which several domains of the application field are described in naturally language. A typical problem description should contain static information as well as dynamic aspects. It should provide information on the environment/domains as well as information/requirements regarding the system itself. Apart from the problem description, information on the application domain can come from other sources e.g. the analyst's knowledge. Such information should be marked so that it can always be identified if required. It should be possible to trace the sources of information at all times.

The aim of the requirements determination process is to analyze the problem description for requirements in order to obtain a better understanding of the system to be built and the environment in which it will be run. The objective is to find, extract and classify requirements and to identify possible actors who will interact with the system. These may be human beings, hardware or software systems. This activity should lead to a rethinking of the system's feasibility as well as of the system itself. Once requirements have been found and extracted, they should be checked for inconsistency, incompleteness, redundancy and ambiguity.

As the development process [Som01] continues, new requirements may and will arise. Already defined requirements may have to be abandoned or modified. All these changes have to be checked and documented in the requirements documentation as well as in the Data Dictionary. All subsequent models of the process should be checked against the requirements. The output of *requirements determination* is the *requirements definition*. Davis [Dav93] makes a distinction between requirements definition and requirements specification. Whereas definition is a high-level abstract description of requirements, specification is a more detailed description of what the system should do, i.e. the software specification, which is presented in the next chapter. To demonstrate the process of requirements determination we use the DAISY-Soft case study. DAISY-Soft can be found in the Appendix A.

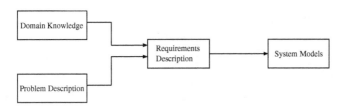

Figure 7.1: The Requirements Determination process

7.2 Extracting Requirements from the Problem Description

The very first thing to do is to read the problem description carefully. It should be structured in such a way that it is easy to identify all domains of the application domain that are involved, directly or indirectly, with the problem to be solved. Thus, everything that is important for the requirements must occur in some part of the application domain.

A domain can be thought of as a separate world inhabited by its own conceptual entities or objects. We distinguish between two domains: the application domain – the environment – and the system domain. The application domain lies where the customer's requirements are, the system domain is where the solution of the problem is by interacting in some way with the application domain. One can think of the application domain as what is given, and of the system domain as what has to be constructed.

There are two different kinds of domain areas:

Dynamic domains are those where things can happen and change. Anything that affects the state of the system domain from outside is dynamic.

Static domains are those where no changes occur. These are mostly those domains that neither interact with the system nor are part of the system itself.

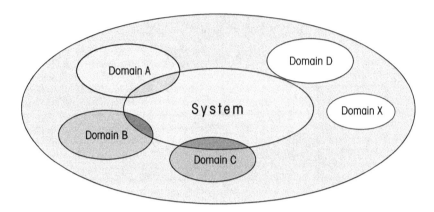

Figure 7.2: Application domain of the system

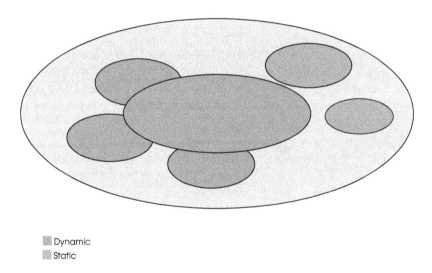

Figure 7.3: Static and dynamic domains from the system's point of view in the application domain

7.2.1 Defining Domains

The aim of this activity is to define different domains that are directly or indirectly involved in the system. One could argue that the indirect areas are of no interest for the system. However, as has already been stated, in order to capture the requirements and obtain an understanding of the problem to be solved, it is necessary to have information about the domains. And it is also important to have this knowledge for the subsequent analysis steps, e.g. for tracing or system validation. The problem description is the main source for extracting information on different domains from the application domain. An example of how to define the domains is given in the next section.

Example: Problem Description of DAISY-Soft

DAISY-Soft treats the two directions of an Underground line as two separate lines. It must have knowledge of the topology of the respective underground line. A line as a software structure consists of a directed sequence of stations with two unique stations, namely the start-terminal and the terminus. Lines and Stations are objects with well-defined attributes, like the name of the station. Moreover, the relationship between the stations and lines must be designed in such a way that each can in turn have attributes. Each line should be seen as a separate line, independent of all the other lines. Each line has its own track, which is not used by any other lines.

The driver is responsible for stopping and restarting the train at the stations, and is also responsible for opening and closing the train doors.

DAISY-Soft must also take into account that each train will be placed on the track by the Monitor Control System (*MCS*). Specific information on the position of the train on the track and its state must be recorded. Finally, for each station train information must be administered. The *Train-info* contains an identification of the train as well as its position and expected arrival time.

The administration of *Train-info* includes

- the generation of new info when the *MCS* establishes a train

- the deletion of info when the train leaves a station or reaches the terminus

- the updating of all info on the subsequent stations when a train leaves a station

If a train stops unexpectedly, all preceding trains are treated normally. All the following trains are given special treatment. Instead of the arrival times being displayed, a change has to be made in the form of a special announcement like "irregular train traffic" on the *train-infos*.

Every clock at the underground station is updated by a central clock ensuring that all clocks show the same time.

At regular intervals, the station's *Information Board* fetches the train info from the system.

DAISY-Soft is not responsible for coding of the Information Board – it merely supplies the information – or for correcting or changing timetables, avoiding collisions, dealing with disasters or the like. Nor is it responsible for providing train information in a specific order.

7.2.1.1   Identifying Relevant Domain Areas in the Application Domain

The first step is to identify all domains of the application domain, including the system domain. The system domain is a subset of the application domain.

In the case of Daisy, we have the following domains in the application domain:

- Monitor Control System (MCS)

- Driver

- Information Board

- Underground

- Clock

- Train

- Line

- TrainInfo

- Station

In our case the system domain consists of subsets of domains of Train, Line, Station and TrainInfo. The next step is to classify all identified domains into static and dynamic domains.

MCS, Driver and Information Board are dynamic domains, whereas *Clock and Underground* are static domains. *Train, Line, Station and TrainInfo* are also dynamic domains. Dynamic domain areas are those that belong to the optative moods. The static domains are the indicative moods (cf. Chapter 3).

After naming the different domain areas which are part of the application domain. The entry *identifier* of the requirement template is a combination of the abbreviation of the domain (first two characters) and a unique number. It is easy to identify domain requirements by their identifier.

7.2.2 Extracting Requirements

The next step is to extract the requirements of the domain area from the problem description. Having done that, we then look for the system requirements. Next, we find and note the statements for which the system is not responsible. This gives us the freedom to design the next models of the process. One does not start questioning during the developing process whether that information should be part of system or not. Whenever possible, requirements should be expressed in a formally descriptive way. When all the requirements have been collected, classified and formally described, the requirements definition should be revisited to see if they are all correct. In the very first instantiation of requirements determination, it is important to extract as much information as possible from the problem description. Still, in the ongoing analysis process, new requirements emerge. With the very first models of the method, e.g. the Use Case Model, Domain Class Model and Timeline Model, greater changes in the requirement's definition are likely.

7.2.2.1 Example: Extracting Requirements from the Domains

Domain: MCS

1. Provides train_number and line_number when train is established at the start-terminal of the line.

2. Establish train at start-terminal of that line.

3. MCS stops train on track in case of emergency and informs driver of that train.

4. Removes train at terminus when all passengers have left the train.

5. Removes train and informs the driver of the train.

6. After an interruption the driver gets informed that journey of train can continue on this line.

Domain: Driver

1. Continues journey after regular stop at station.

2. Stops and continues journey of train on track (in communication with the MCS).

3. MSC given the permission to continue journey between two stations.

4. Makes announcements on the train during journey.

5. Opens and closes train doors while train stops at or between stations.

Domain: Information Board

1. Has limited space for information on the Information Board.

2. Asks for train information from DAISY-Soft at regular intervals.

3. Updates train information on the Information Board at certain intervals.

Domain: Clock

1. Continuously updates the time at Station, Train, MCS and Information Board.

7.2.2.2   Extracting System Requirements from the System Domain

1. The system must treat the two directions of an underground line as two separate lines.

2. The system must treat two stations (start-terminal and terminus) as special stations on the line.

3. The system must know that all stations following the start-terminal on the line are the subsequent stations of that line.

4. The system must treat the start-terminal differently to the subsequent stations, when train leaves the station.

5. The system shall update train information for all subsequent stations on the line when train leaves the station.

6. The system shall delete train information when train has been removed at terminus (and only then).

7. The system shall generate special information for the subsequent stations when train has been stopped between two stations.

8. The system shall update the train information for all subsequent stations when train leaves the station.

9. Once the Information Board of the station has collected the information from the system, the system shall delete this information.

7.2.2.3 Non-Responsible Statements

It is as important to define for what the system is not responsible, as it is to define for what the system is responsible. We call this **the Non-Responsible Statement**. The requirements it contains are not system requirements but they can be and are important for the system [Som01].

1. All train numbers are unique and are generated by the MCS.

2. All line numbers are unique and are generated by the MCS.

3. The timetable of trains is controlled by the MCS.

4. DAISY-Soft is responsible for neither the information boards nor the timetable.

5. DAISY-Soft is not responsible for the correct timetable of trains.

6. DAISY-Soft is not responsible for train collisions or any other disasters.

7.2.3 Classify Extracted Requirements and the Non-responsible Statements

When the requirements have been extracted from their domains, system domain and the non responsible statements, each requirement should be classified according to its domain and type. Such classifications help to identify classes of requirements.

7.2.3.1 Types

In this section, the set of types of requirements is described and defined. At this stage of development we do not consider any nonfunctional requirements. There are three different types of requirements:

Definition: Fact
are requirements of the environment that describe the precondition of the application domain and thus of the system. They express things that are always true

of the domain, regardless of the implementation of the software system. A fact can either be a constraint or an assumption. Facts are the general expression of environmental requirements, which can have a direct or indirect effect on the system to be built.

Example:

Requirement of domain *Information Board*:
Has limited space for information on the Information Board is of the type *Fact* because it is a piece of information that does not have a direct impact on the system.

Definition: Constraint
are requirements of the environment that describe the application domain and have an direct impact on the system. The system must respond directly to the constraints.

Example:

Requirement of domain *MCS*: *MCS stops train on track in case of emergency and informs Driver of that train* is of the type *constraint* because the system has to react by generating new information with a special announcement. The corresponding *system requirement* to this requirement is: *The system must generate special information for the subsequent stations when train has been stopped between two stations.*

Definition: System
are those requirements that describe the functionality of the system to be built.

Example:

The system must have knowledge of the topology of the respective underground line. This requirement expresses this knowledge of an underground line and describes a line as a software structure.

The system must treat the two directions of an underground line as two separate lines.

7.2.3.2   Non-responsible Statements

The non-responsible statements are not requirements of the system.

Definition: Non-Responsible Statements
are statements for which the system is not responsible. They are therefore not part of the system but describe a certain kind of property of the application domain. Non-Responsible Statements can be identified and thus classified by their domain.

Example:

A non-responsible statement of Daisy-Soft:

All train numbers are unique and are generated by the MCS.

7.3 Describing Requirements in a More Formal Way

Whenever it is possible to describe requirements in a more formal way, as a *formal statement*, this should be done. One must know that not all requirements can be described formally. The entry of the requirements definition template *Formal* is therefore optional.

Definition: Formal Statement gives a formal description of a term that may be used by other models of the method, e.g. Operation Model, Formal Description.

Describing requirements as a formal statement at this early stage of software development has its advantages for the models later on in the process, e.g. the Operation Model and Formal Description. We use the Z notation [1] or predicate logic to express formal statements of a requirement. Both models, *Operation Model* and *Formal Description*, use the same language as the formal statement. As the formal statements are suitable as environment invariants and class invariants for the *Formal Description*, the inclusion of the formal statements is easier than if the language for formal statement were different from the language of the Formal Description. In the case of different languages, matching the expression of formal statement would need checking before the expression could be integrated into the *Formal Description*.

Examples of requirements which are described as a formal statement:

Example of a domain requirement

Requirement MCS_1: MCS provides a train_number and line_number when train is established at the start-terminal.

$$\forall\, trains : Train, l : Line \mid \exists\, t : trains \bullet (t, l) \in established$$

Example of a system requirement

Requirement Sys_1: The system must treat the two directions of an underground line as two separate lines.

$$\exists\, undergound\_line : Line \leftrightarrow Line \mid first(underground\_line) \neq second(underground\_line)$$

A requirement for which a formal statement is not adequate:

---

[1]Object-Z is an extension of Z; we could also say we use Object-Z.

A requirement should not be expressed in a formal way when it is either a qualitative statement or a non-responsible statement.

For example, the requirement *Has limited space for information on the Information Board* has no effect on the system. When we look at the non-responsible statement: *DAISY-Soft is not responsible for train collisions or any other disasters*, it is important to know who will be in charge if a disaster occurs, but it is of no relevance for understanding of the system.

7.4   Linking Requirements to Models of the Metho

Linking requirements to the system models increases the traceability of the system. The explicit link between the requirements and the models makes it easier to cross check models and associated requirements. The Data Dictionary is the repository that keeps records of the requirements and all modelling elements of the models throughout the software development process. Each requirement must be recorded in the Data Dictionary, e.g.

Name	Kind	Description	Source
MCS_1	Requirement	The Monitor Control System must deliver a train and line number	Requirements Description, Use Case Model, Domain Class Model, etc.

Besides the Data Dictionary, the Use Case Model and the Domain Class Model are artefacts for gluing requirements to the modelling elements. In the Use Case Model, these modelling elements are the use cases and actors (cf. Figure 7.4). Requirements are attached to the use case and actors as tagged values (cf. Figure 7.1).

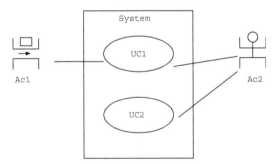

Figure 7.4: Use Case

	UC1	UC2
Ac1	Req_3, Req_4	Req_5
Ac2		Req_1, Req_2

Table 7.1: Requirement links

The Use Case Model may be the first model in the method where requirements are checked for consistency . In the Domain Class Model, the modelling elements for linking requirements are the classes. The Domain Class Model describes the static view of the application domain, where besides the requirements also the **non-responsible statements** also are listed in the corresponding classes. To link requirements in the Domain Class Model, a third compartment of the modelling element class is extended for identification of the requirements (cf. Figure 7.5).

Figure 7.5: Compartment extension of a class for linking requirements

Here is an example of how the requirements are glued to the classes of the Domain Class Model (cf. Figure 7.6).

Figure 7.6: Example: Linking requirements in a Class

A complete example of linking requirements to other models of the method can be found in Appendix A.

7.5 Requirements Description

The result of the *requirements determination process* is the *Requirements Description*. It is a collection of all requirements and non-responsible statements of the system and its environment. This document should be consistent with the entries of the Data Dictionary.

The complete requirements for the system consist of the system requirements and the domain requirements:

Requirements = system requirements ∪ domain requirements

Requirements Description = non-responsible statements ∪ requirements

Req-Id	=	*Identifier*
Type	=	*Type*
Rational	=	*Textual description*
Formal	=	*Formal statement, this field is optional*
Links	=	*List of links to other models for tracing*

Figure 7.7: A requirement template

Req-Id	=	MCS_1
Type	=	Fact
Rational	=	MCS provides a unique train_number and a unique line_number when train is established at the start-terminal.
Formal	=	$\forall\, trains : Train, lines : Line \mid \exists\, t : trains, l : lines \bullet (t, l) \in established$
Links	=	Domain Class Model, Use Case Model

Figure 7.8: Example of a domain requirement

Req-Id	=	Sys_2
Type	=	System
Rational	=	The system must treat two stations (start-terminal and terminus) as special stations on the line
Formal	=	$\exists\, s1 : Station, sn : Station, l : Line \bullet l.start - terminal = s1 \wedge l.terminus = sn$
Links	=	Use Case Model, Domain Class Model

Figure 7.9: Example of a system requirement

The templates shown here contain only the most important entries for managing requirements. An expanded template with more entries can be found in Appendix

Req-Id	=	*Non-resp Identifier*
Rational	=	*Textual description*
Domain	=	*Domain*

Figure 7.10: A non-responsible template

Req-Id	=	Non_resp01
Rational	=	The trains timetable of is controlled by the MCS system
Domain	=	MCS system

Figure 7.11: Example of a non-responsible statement

C. This requirements template is designed for a tool, where certain entries are made automatically.

Chapter 8

Enhancement — Towards Formal Specification

In this chapter, we describe an additional step that goes further in providing consistency for the developed design: systematic translation of the two main results of the process, the Operation Model and the Object Interaction Model, into the formal specification language Object-Z [DR00, Smi00, BK03]. This additional step is intended to form a fruitful transition from the "soft" to the "hard" side of software engineering. We gain two things from this additional translation. Firstly, we should note that the Operation Model represents a much rougher view of the system, in that it models the entire system using just one global state, whereas the Object Interaction Model splits up the functionality as well as the state into the scopes of various system classes. Hence, the Object Interaction Model can be seen as a *refinement* of the Operation Model. However, since we are using the formal language Object-Z, for which a well-defined refinement exists [DB01], this refinement can be formally verified. Secondly, as we derive a formal specification from the semi formal UML design constructed by the Fusion process, we can use Object-Z refinement again to extend consistency checking beyond the design process: any implementation of the Class Interface Model must again be a refinement of the derived Object-Z specification.

8.1   The Process

We use a simple example, a savings account, to demonstrate the process. A more complex example is given in Appendix A.

As an example of a System Class Model of a very simple savings account, consider the diagram shown in Figure 8.1.

The System Class Model finalizes the static analysis of the system. As a fi-

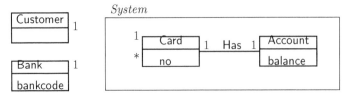

Figure 8.1: System Class Model for savings account

nal result for the dynamic part, the information gathered in the Use Case Model, Timeline Model and Life Cycle Model is combined into the *Operation Model*. The Operation Model consists of a set of operation schemata. Operation schemata are, although in their particular incarnation novel to the UML, merely a composition of UML tagged values. The values tagged together are: Name, Description, Inputs, Reads, Changes, Sends, Precondition and Postcondition. In other words, an operation schema contains the operation's name, its informal description and inputs. Furthermore, such a schema defines the objects and associations from which the operation reads and on which it writes, further specifying concrete conditions on those objects using a with-clause followed by a formal condition in Z. The pre- and postconditions tagged with an operation schema may define formal conditions about the operation using Z as a logical language. The formulas defined here may range over all values within the bound of the current operation schema.

For example, the Operation Model for the bank system contains a system operation that enables a customer to pay into his/her account.

Operation	=	deposit
Description	=	A customer pays an amount into his/her account.
Input	=	$amnt : \mathbb{N}, acc : \mathbb{N}$
Reads	=	$\underline{c : Card}$ **with** $c.no = acc, Has$
Changes	=	$\underline{a : Account}$ **with** $(c, a) \in Has$
Sends	=	$\underline{: Customer} : \{trans\_ok\}$
Pre	=	**true**
Post	=	$a.balance' = a.balance + amnt \wedge$ **is_sent** $\{trans\_ok\}$

The system needs the amount and the account number as inputs. In order to deposit the amount into the right account, the appropriate card must be read and the corresponding account is changed. The changes to the balance are expressed in the postcondition of the operation schema. As a system event, a message is sent to the customer to inform him/her about the successful transaction.

To withdraw an amount from an account, the corresponding system operation *withdraw* must first check whether the balance in the account for this card is sufficient. The transaction may be carried out only if the amount to be withdrawn does not not exceed the balance in the account, otherwise the balance is not changed and a corresponding message is sent to the customer.

Operation	=	withdraw
Description	=	A customer wishes to withdraw an amount from his/her account. If the balance in the account is sufficient, the amount is paid out.
Input	=	$amnt : \mathbb{N}, acc : \mathbb{N}$
Reads	=	$c : \underline{Card}$ **with** $c.nr = acc, Has$
Changes	=	$a : \underline{Account}$ **with** $(c, a) \in Has$
Sends	=	$: \underline{Customer} : \{trans\_ok\}, \{too\_much\}$
Pre	=	**true**
Post	=	$(a.balance - amnt \geq 1 \Rightarrow$ $a.balance' = a.balance - amnt \wedge \textbf{is\_sent}\ \{trans\_ok\}) \wedge$ $(a.balance - amnt < 1 \Rightarrow$ $a.balance' = a.balance \wedge \textbf{is\_sent}\ \{too\_much\})$

The design must be consistent with the analysis. In particular, for all system operations defined during the analysis, the *Object Interaction Model* must define *object interaction graphs* describing the execution of the system operation on theobjects in the system. To this end, the object interaction graphs introduce new operations: the graphs are UML collaborations, defining message flows in a sequential order using numbers. The object interaction starts from an actor executing the system operation as a message to an object called the *controller* of that system operation. The controller delegates the initial system operation to so-called *collaborators* , objects of the system that are associated with the controller. Here delegation may be introduced: the initial task initiated by the controller can likewise be deferred by the collaborators to other objects they are associated with, thereby creating submessage flows. For the sake of consistency, it must be checked that all objects corresponding with each other are connected in the System Class Model by associations. Alongside the objects, UML annotations with { } may be used to describe the selection of this particular object or to annotate pre- or postconditions for the method calls contained in the messages.

The object interaction graph of the operation deposit is shown in Figure 8.2. An additional feature of object interactions is conditional branching. It is enabled using guards. This is illustrated in Figure 8.3 where the operation withdraw is described by its object interaction. Other typical cases of object interactions are

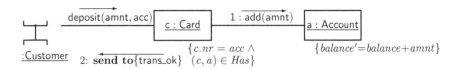

Figure 8.2: Object interaction for deposit

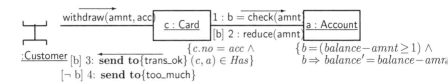

Figure 8.3: Object interaction for withdraw

sequential composition of message flows, delegation, and messages to collections of objects. We illustrate these when defining the translation process in Section 8.2.2.

8.2 Schematic Translation into Object-Z

8.2.1 Operation Model

We begin by outlining how the translation works, and then go on to present a formal translation schema.

All system operations of the Operation Model are placed as Object-Z operation schemata in one Object-Z class, called *System*.

Separate classes (data structures) are declared for all objects of the **Reads** and **Changes** parts. All attributes of the declared classes are defined in the *state schema* of the respective class. The precise content of these classes is later derived when translating the object interactions in the second step.

Declarations of objects in the **Reads** and **Changes** parts are transformed into local declarations of the *state schema* of the class *System*.

The content of the **sends** parts becomes the output parameters of the corresponding operation schemata of *System*.

Pre- and postconditions are translated one-to-one into the predicate parts of the corresponding Object-Z operation schemata of *System*.

The Inputs of the system operations become input parameters of the operation schemata.

Generally speaking, an operation schema for the system operation $sysop_i$ has the following form:

Operation	=	$sysop_i$
Description	=	...
Input	=	$i_1 : I_1, \ldots, i_n : I_n$
Reads	=	$r_1 : R_1$ **with** $P_{R_1}, \ldots, r_k : R_k$ **with** P_{R_k}
Changes	=	$c_1 : C_1$ **with** $P_{C_1}, \ldots, c_l : C_l$ **with** P_{C_l}
Sends	=	$\underline{} : A_1 : \{s_1\}, \ldots, \underline{} : A_m : \{s_m\}$
Pre	=	P_{pre}
Post	=	P_{post}

The variables P_x are predicates that may contain all local variables, the inputs i_j, the reads and changes r_j and c_j, and the messages s_j. The general translation method for the Operation Model produces one class $System_A$, whose state schema entails sets of objects of all reads and changes declarations for all system operations. The dots indicate where additional system operations may add to the state. Class $System_A$ contains one operation schema for each system operation. In one step of translation, the above operation schema produces the following portion of the system class.

$\underline{\quad System_A \quad}$

$rs_1 : \mathbb{P}\, R_1, \ldots rs_k : \mathbb{P}\, R_k$
$cs_1 : \mathbb{P}\, C_1, \ldots cs_l : \mathbb{P}\, C_l$
$\vdots$

$\underline{\quad sysop_i \quad}$
$\Delta(cs_1, \ldots, cs_n)$
$i_1? : I_1, \ldots, i_n? : I_n$
$m! : Report$

$\exists\ r_1 : rs_1, \ldots r_k : rs_k, c_1 : cs_1, \ldots c_l : cs_l \bullet$
$\qquad P_{R_1} \wedge \ldots \wedge P_{R_k} \wedge$
$\qquad P_{C_1} \wedge \ldots \wedge P_{C_l} \wedge$
$\qquad P_{pre} \wedge$
$\qquad P_{post}[m! = s_i / \textbf{is\_sent}\ (s_i)]$

Note that the **is_sent** parts are replaced by corresponding Object-Z definitions of output parameter $m!$ for each message s_j.

Each object listed in the reads and send part is translated into a class (abstract data structures). These classes are complemented by methods in the next translation period.

$$
\begin{array}{|l|}
\hline
\;C_l \\[4pt]
\hline
\quad co_1 : Co_1 \\
\quad \vdots \\
\quad co_n : Co_n \\
\hline
\end{array}
$$

8.2.2   Object Interaction Model

In this section, we define the translation of the Object Interaction Model into Object-Z using a formal description of the possible cases of collaborations such as occur in object interaction graphs. Compared to the Object-Z representation of the Operation Model, the translation of the Object Interaction Model has a refined class structure: the system operations are now distributed to the controller classes rather than being contained in the system class.

Method calls of the messages in the object interactions contribute as new operation schemata to the classes that resulted from the **Reads** and **Changes** parts in the previous step.

An object of a collection must be created through a schema. The creation is expressed by a local declaration of the object. The nonexistence of the object in the aggregate is expressed by the existential operator and is added with the *union operator* to the aggregate (cf. Section A.9.1).

Deletion of an object of a collection must be done through a schema. The deletion is expressed by a local declaration of the object. The existence of object is expressed by the existential operator and the proof that the object exists in the aggregate and is removed by the *hide operator* of the aggregate (cf. Section A.9.1)[1]

The structure of the invocation given by the messages is incarnated into operation definitions in the schema calculus of Object-Z residing in the controller classes.

The distribution of methods to classes is guided by the direction of the arrows above the messages of the object interaction: the arrow points towards the server

---

[1] Note: It should be emphasized that Object-Z does not address the creation or destruction of objects per se: it is asserted that objects always exist [DR00].

class, so the server must provide the corresponding method.

The following translation rules must be applied in combination in order to provide a complete translation of a design. Additional features, like attributes, contained in the System Class Model must be added to the state schema in a final pass of the translation process. Relations in the system class of the Operation Model are translated into class references or links in the Object-Z specification of the respective class.

Internal Methods with Parameters

In cases where the newly defined method calls act with parameter passing (cf. Figure 8.4), we represent these parameters in the translation by the concept of input and output variables of Object-Z.

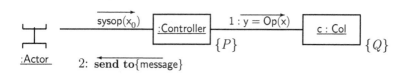

Figure 8.4: Method calls and parameterization

The class *Controller* representing the controller has a reference to an instance c of the collaborator class. The system operation sysop resides in the controller class, but is implemented using the method Op of the server class Col. The input x_0 to the system operation may already contain the input x to the new method Op. However, new input parameters may also be specified in conditions P or Q. Nevertheless, the inputs and outputs may be simply translated using the scope enrichment of Object-Z, because parameters with identical names are matched and differing parameters are unified according to the naming conventions in Object-Z.

The tagged condition P, containing a **with** clause used as a selection condition, and possibly pre- and postconditions for the delegated method, is represented by a predicate in an Object-Z scope enrichment of *sysop*.

$$
\begin{array}{|l}
\hline
\;\textit{Controller} \;\underline{\hspace{6cm}} \\
\;\; \begin{array}{|l}
\hline
\; c : Col \\
\hline
\end{array} \\
\; sysop \mathrel{\widehat{=}} [\Delta(c)\; x_0? : Type(x_0), m! : Report \mid \\
\qquad\qquad\quad P[self/s] \wedge m! = message] \bullet c.Op \\
\hline
\end{array}
$$

The notation *Type* indicates that the translation contains the actual type of the parameters. Although we use single variables here, the general case of several inputs and outputs is captured as well, as their types may be unified in one product type. The Object-Z element *self* denoting this instance of class *Controller* must replace the named object representing the actual controller of the interaction.

The message **message** sent to the actor is added as an additional output parameter $m!$, defined as an enumeration type

$$Report ::= message \mid \ldots$$

the dots indicating that this message type is dynamically extended by messages representing system events during the translation process. To be able to incorporate the Fusion message passing into the Object-Z representation, a further dummy class *Actor* is added to the specification. Although not part of the system classes it is relevant for modelling the communication with the environment.

Actor _____

$s : Controller$

$sysop \mathrel{\widehat{=}} s.sysop$

Finally, the class *Col* contains an op-schema representing the operation *Op*. Parameter passing is straightforwardly mapped to the input and output variables of Object-Z, inputs being indicated by ? and outputs by !. The tagged condition Q, specifying conditions on the selection of the collaborator object and the parameters, is added as the predicate of the op-schema.

Col _____

  Op _____
  $x? : Type(\mathsf{x})$
  $y! : Type(\mathsf{y})$
  _____
  $Q[self/c]$

Conditional Control Flow

A very important case of an object interaction is where the message flow is conditional on the Boolean result of a first message, as depicted in Figure 8.5. In terms of the state, the translation resembles the sequential composition. However, to define the system operation in the controller class, we first define two separate functions for the two cases that are combined using the schema calculus.

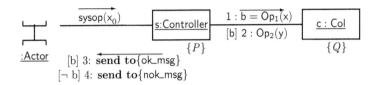

Figure 8.5: Conditional control flow

__ *Controller* _____

    | *c* : *Col*

$sysop\_ok \mathrel{\widehat{=}} [\Delta(c), x? : Type(x_0), b? : \mathbb{B} \mid$
$\qquad\qquad b? \wedge P[self/s] \wedge m! = ok\_msg] \bullet c.Op_2$
$sysop\_nok \mathrel{\widehat{=}} [x? : Type(x_0), b? : \mathbb{B} \mid \neg b? \wedge P[self/s] \wedge m! = nok\_msg]$
$sysop \mathrel{\widehat{=}} c.Op_1 \mathbin{\fatsemi} (sysop\_ok \mathbin{[\!]} sysop\_nok)$

Sequential Composition

The next typical case of an object interaction is a sequence of method calls from the same controller to a number of collaborators (cf. Figure 8.6).

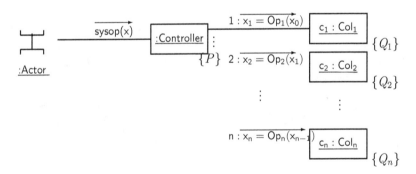

Figure 8.6: Sequences of method calls

This sequentially composed system operation can be modelled using the sequential composition operator of Object-Z's schema calculus. We have already integrated the translation step from the previous section, i.e. the parameter passing between controller and collaborator, but have left out the Fusion message part in order not to obscure the exposition.

$$\underline{\quad Controller\quad}$$

$c1 : Col_1$

$\vdots$

$c_n : Col_n$

$sysop \mathrel{\widehat{=}} [\Delta(c_1, \ldots, c_n)\ x? : Type(\mathsf{x}) \mid P[self/s]] \bullet c_1.Op_1 \, {}^{\mathrm{o}}_{\mathrm{g}} \ldots {}^{\mathrm{o}}_{\mathrm{g}}\ c_n.Op_n$

As before, the operations $Op_1, \ldots, Op_n$ get their respective inputs and outputs. Since the controller object demands the services $Op_1, \ldots, Op_n$ from the collaborators, we know that they must provide the new functionality and can take over the conditions tagged to the object interactions.

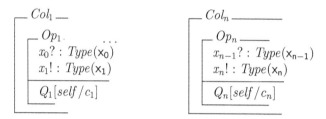

Delegation

A very important case of object interaction is the delegation of a method call. A collaborator delegates a message to another class. The collaborator thereby becomes a subcontroller using other classes as collaborators, as depicted in Figure 8.7. For the sake of clarity, we omit parameters and system events, but these may be integrated here following the previous translation schemata. The translation

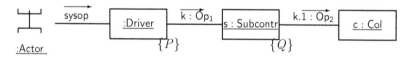

Figure 8.7: Delegation of method calls

resembles the sequential composition. However, at the controller level we have

$$\underline{\quad Controller\quad}$$

$s : Subcontr$

$sysop \mathrel{\widehat{=}} [\Delta(s) \mid P[self[s_0]]] \bullet s.Op_1$

where the delegated operation now resides in the subcontroller.

$\underline{\quad Subcontr\quad\rule{6cm}{0.4pt}}$

$\quad c : Col$
$\rule{7cm}{0.4pt}$
$\quad Op \mathrel{\widehat{=}} [\Delta(c) \mid Q[self/s]] \bullet c.Op_2$

The operation Op is, as before, contained in the corresponding collaborator classes.

Collections of Objects in Interactions

A special case that may occur in object interactions are collections of objects. A message is sent to the collection of all objects of one class rather than to just one instance of that class. This case is illustrated in Figure 8.8. This collaboration

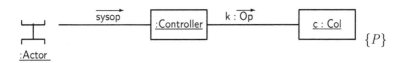

Figure 8.8: Method calls and collections

means that message Op is sent to all objects c of class Col such that P holds.

Fortunately, Object-Z offers distributed operators in its schema calculus, representing generalizations for finite sets of objects that may be employed for this case. As there is no order in the calls to the objects contained in the collection, we can employ the schema calculus operator $\wedge$ instead of $\mathbin{\substack{\circ\\\circ}}$. The translation of the controller class is

$\underline{\quad Controller\quad\rule{6cm}{0.4pt}}$

$\quad cc : \mathbb{F}\; Col$
$\rule{7cm}{0.4pt}$
$\quad sysop \mathrel{\widehat{=}} \bigwedge[c : cc \mid P[self/s]] \bullet c.Op$

Clearly, the translation of class Col contains, as before, an op-schema for Op. The previous translation methods also apply to this case when they are combined with parameter passing, delegation or sequential composition.

8.2.3 Example

The schematic process of translation into Object-Z described in the previous section is now illustrated by the running example from the bank case study.

Translation of the Operation Model

First, we show the translation for the analysis. The messages are collected in an enumeration type *Report*.

$$Report ::= trans\_ok \mid too\_much \ldots$$

The translation of the operations *deposit* and *withdraw* leads to the definition of the single class $System_A$.

$$
\begin{array}{|l}
\hline
\_System_A _____ \\
\begin{array}{|l}
\hline
cards : \mathbb{P}\ Card \\
accounts : \mathbb{P}\ Account \\
Has : Card \leftrightarrow Account \\
\hline
\end{array} \\
\begin{array}{|l}
\hline
\_deposit _____ \\
\Delta(a) \\
amnt?, acc? : \mathbb{N} \\
m! : Report \\
\hline
\exists\ c : cards, a : accounts \bullet \\
\quad c.nr = acc?\ \wedge \\
\quad (c, a) \in Has\ \wedge \\
\quad a.balance' = a.balance + amnt?\ \wedge \\
\quad m! = trans\_ok \\
\hline
\end{array} \\
\hline
\end{array}
$$

$$
\begin{array}{|l}
\hline
\;\_withdraw\,\underline{\hspace{8cm}} \\
\;\Delta(a) \\
\;amnt?, acc? : \mathbb{N} \\
\;m! : Report \\
\hline
\;\exists\; c : cards, a : accounts \bullet \\
\quad\;\; c.no = acc?\; \wedge \\
\quad\;\; (c, a) \in Has\; \wedge \\
\quad\;\; (a.balance - amnt? \geq 1 \Rightarrow \\
\qquad\quad a.balance' = a.balance - amnt?\; \wedge\; m! = trans\_ok)\; \wedge \\
\quad\;\; (a.balance - amnt? < 1 \Rightarrow \\
\qquad\quad a.balance' = a.balance\; \wedge\; m! = too\_much) \\
\hline
\end{array}
$$

We define all listed types (Card, Account) in the state schema of the system class *System$_A$* as separate classes (data structures) in Object-Z. These are classes with only a state space but no operations. In Z, we would define these types as basic types, e.g. [Card, Amount]. We will see that when the object interaction graphs are translated, these classes are extended by operations.

$$
\begin{array}{|l}
\hline
\;\_Card\,\underline{\hspace{5cm}} \\
\hline
\;a : Account \\
\;no : \mathbb{N} \\
\hline
\end{array}
\qquad
\begin{array}{|l}
\hline
\;\_Account\,\underline{\hspace{5cm}} \\
\hline
\;balance : \mathbb{N} \\
\hline
\end{array}
$$

Translation of the Object Interactions

The object interactions are translated into the controller *Card* and the collaborator *Account*. The translation for *deposit* uses the scheme for internal methods with parameters; *withdraw* is generated by the same rule plus the one for conditional control flow (cf. Section 8.2.2).

$$
\begin{array}{|l}
\hline
\;\_Card\,\underline{\hspace{8cm}} \\
\hline
\;a : Account \\
\;no : \mathbb{N} \\
\hline
\end{array}
$$

$$\begin{array}{|l}
\hline
\_\_withdraw\_nok_____ \\
amnt? : \mathbb{N} \\
acc? : \mathbb{N} \\
b? : \mathbb{B} \\
m! : Report \\
\hline
self.no = acc? \\
\neg b? \\
m! = too\_much \\
\hline
\end{array}$$

$$deposit \;\widehat{=}\; [\Delta(a)\; amnt?, acc? : \mathbb{N} \mid self.no = acc?] \bullet a.add$$

$$withdraw\_ok \;\widehat{=}\; [\Delta(a)\; amnt?, acc? : \mathbb{N}, b? : \mathbb{B} \mid b? \wedge self.no = acc?$$
$$\wedge\; m! = trans\_ok] \bullet a.reduce$$

$$withdraw \;\widehat{=}\; a.check\_balance \;\mathbin{;}\; (withdraw\_ok \;[\!]\; withdraw\_nok)$$

Note how the additional feature $no : \mathbb{N}$ from the System Class Model is incorporated into the state schema. Actor class and message type definition (identical to the translated Operation Model) are omitted. The combination into a class suitable for refinement is described in the following section.

$$\begin{array}{|l}
\hline
\_\_Account_____ \\
\\
\hline
balance : \mathbb{N} \\
\hline
\\
\_\_add_____ \\
\Delta(balance) \\
amnt? : \mathbb{N} \\
\hline
balance' = balance + amnt? \\
\hline
\\
\_\_check\_balance_____ \\
amnt? : \mathbb{N} \\
b! : \mathbb{B} \\
\hline
b! = (balance - amnt? \geq 0) \\
\hline
\end{array}$$

```
┌─ reduce ─────────────────────────────────────────────┐
│ Δ(balance)                                            │
│ amnt? : ℕ                                             │
│ ├───────────────────────────────────────────────────│
│ balance − amnt? ≥ 0                                   │
│ balance' = balance − amnt?                            │
└───────────────────────────────────────────────────────┘
```

8.2.4 Refinement

The state of the art of refinement in Object-Z is such that single-class refinement is well understood [DB01]. However, structural refinement, i.e. the concept of several classes put together constituting a refinement of a single class, is a current research topic. But structural refinement is exactly what is needed here: the class $System_A$ of the Operation Model is refined by a structure that consists of several controller classes. Fortunately, as we know from a personal communication with Graeme Smith, the author of [Smi00], the following structure is a legal workaround for structural refinement.

In addition to the translation of the classes seen in Section 8.2.2, the representation of the system in Object-Z contains a class $System_D$ that entails sets of references to the controller classes and the associations that have been so far left out of the translation process for object interactions. The state of this class is identical to the state of $System_A$.

```
┌─ System_D ───────────────────────────────────────────┐
│                                                       │
│ ┌───────────────────────────────────────────────────│
│ │ cards : ℙ Card                                      │
│ │ accounts : ℙ Account                                │
│ └───────────────────────────────────────────────────│
└───────────────────────────────────────────────────────┘
```

This final step completes the translation process of the Object Interaction Model. The refinement condition

$$System_A \sqsubseteq System_D$$

enables us to verify that the axiomatic descriptions in the Operation Model conform to their representations in the Object Interaction Model. Hence, Object-Z refinement ensures consistency between analysis and design.

The state schemata of $System_A$ and $System_D$ are identical in most cases. In these cases, the data refinement defined by a retrieve relation connecting abstract and concrete state spaces is the identity. Hence, the verification task for refinement usually boils down to proving operational refinement.

This is the objective we claim to have achieved using the current concept. Fusion/UML is a mature method to guide the process of designing systems. It supports the checking of consistencies within and between the models involved.

8.3 Enrichment of the Derived Object-Z Classes

The presented translation into Object-Z, however, enables the schematic derivation of a formal specification. The formal specification reflects the results of the design. It enables the consistency check between analysis and design *via* refinement and also the verification of system implementations using again Object-Z refinement.

8.3.1 The Init State Schema

The initial state schema *INIT* defines the initial states of a class and appears after the state schema and before any operation. The declaration accessible to *INIT* is the state schema of the class. The state variables and constants of the class are available in the environment in which it is interpreted. Unlike in Z, where *init* is an operation, in Object-Z it consists of a predicate and is therefore expressed in terms of unprimed variables.

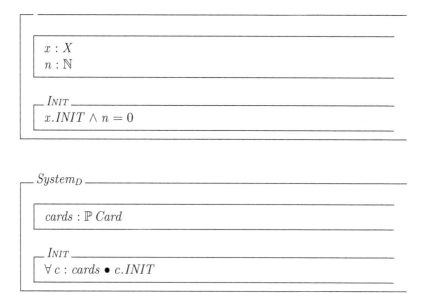

The initial schema of Card is

$\underline{\quad Card\quad}$

$a : Account$
$nr : \mathbb{N}$

$\underline{\quad INIT\quad}$
$a.INIT \wedge nr = 0$

$\ldots$

for the class Account

$\underline{\quad Account\quad}$

$balance : \mathbb{N}$

$\underline{\quad INIT\quad}$
$balance = 0$

$\ldots$

8.3.2 Class Invariants

One further enrichment of the classes adds the class invariants that have been described during requirements determination. For this example, one requirement for the account is: the balance of the account must never be below zero. The formal statement of this is: balance ≥ 0.

$\underline{\quad Account\quad}$

$balance : \mathbb{N}$

$balance \geq 0$

$\ldots$

Chapter 9

$Fusion_B$ – The Extended Fusion/UML Method

The essential property of a method is that, when applied to the right problem and used by the right people (i.e. people with the necessary level of competence), the method will, with a high degree of probability and with a predictable amount of resources, lead to a solution of the problem.

Brio90

In this chapter, we describe the $Fusion_B$ process and its models. We show how the new models and their subprocesses are integrated into the process and the models of the previous Fusion/UML method (cf. Part ??).

9.1 $Fusion_B$ Process

The software developer is guided through the analysis and design process, from requirements determination to formal definition. Several different models for designing software are developed. They are partially transformed from one model to the next and checked for consistency.

With the extension to the Fusion/UML method, the method has been given a new name $Fusion_B$. The figure 9.1 gives an overview of the new process.

Step 1 *Requirements Determination* deals with the extraction of requirements from the problem description for the new system and its environment. The result is the specification of all requirements in the *Requirements Description*.

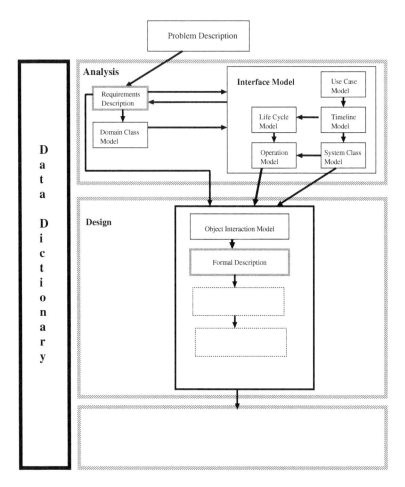

Figure 9.1: **The *Fusion$_B$* Process**

Step 2 Communication at a high level of abstraction between the role of the user and the system is specified by means of a *Use Case Model*. The result is a set of disjoint function groups of the system. Linking requirements to use cases andactors.

Step 3 Objects and concepts within the problem domain are described in a *Domain Class Model* using object-oriented Entity-Relationship modelling. The result is a static structure model of the application domain. The modelling element class is extended to a third compartment for linking requirements and the non-responsible statements. The requirements are linked to the corresponding classes.

Steps 2 and 3 must not be executed strictly sequentially because their views are supplementary and do not overlap.

Step 4 Each use case is refined by scenarios in the form of timeline diagrams. Timeline diagrams are annotated as *sequence diagrams* in the UML style. The modelling elements are system operations and system events. The Use Case Model and the Timeline Model form the system interface.

As a result of the fixed user communication, in Step 5 the boundary between the environment and the system inside the (static) *Domain Class Model*is specified. The result is the *System Class Model*. This step requires the previous steps (1, 2 and 3).

Step 6 includes all identified system operations for a global system behaviour. It is specified in a *Life Cycle Model* using regular expressions. Allsystem operations and system events must be identified in the model. Steps 3 and 4 are prerequisites for this step.

In Step 7, the semantics of each single system operation are specified in as much detail as possible using predicate logic. This results in a so-called operation schema. The combination of these forms the *Operation Model*. The *Life Cycle Model*, *Timeline Model* and *System Class Model* constitute the most important steps in the whole of the analysis phase. From the Operation Model an Object-Z class called *System* and various type classes – data structures – are specified.

In Step 8, each single operation schema is transformed into an object interaction graph. The object interaction graph describes the message flow of the involved objects of the system operation. The object interaction graphs form the *Object Interaction Model*.

In Step 9, the Object-Z class *System* consisting of operations and its state, which was built from the *Operation Model*, is refined to the objects (Object-Z classes) involved in the system. Then the *class invariants* – which come from the *Requirements Description* and the initialization of the classes, the *INIT* operation – are added to the respective Object-Z classes.

In Step 10, the last two models are designed according to Fusion/UML. These models, the *Reference Model* and *Class Interface Model*, are dealt with in Part II, Chapter 6.

The *Data Dictionary* is the central reference glossary in *Fusion$_B$*. All identifiers that are modelling elements (e.g. requirements, use case, actors, classes, associations, attributes, roles, system operations, system events, etc.) are entries in the Data Dictionary. Since the Data Dictionary includes the definition of each individual item there is – at least informally – a semantic consistency of all models. The Data Dictionary also serves as a means for tracing requirements through all models of the method.

9.1.1 Analysis

From the user's point of view, analysis involves understanding and describing external behaviour and its consistencies; contradictions should be detected and diminished. Consideration of the implementation does not form part of this phase.

9.1.1.1 Requirements Determination

Requirements determination is the first activity in the analysis phase of the software process. The purpose of requirements determination is to provide a narrative definition of functional and other requirements that the stakeholders expect to hold in the implemented and deployed system. In *Fusion$_B$*, requirements are extracted from the problem description and the domain knowledge, which form the input for the method. The problem description can be seen as the result of the elicitation process. The output of requirements determination is the *Requirements Description*. It is this model which contains all checked requirements and links to the subsequent models of the method.

How to Obtain Requirements from a Problem Description:

1. identify domain areas of the application domain

2. identify requirements that describe the environment

3. classify requirements of the domains (facts and constraints)

4. classify system requirements and non-responsible statements

5. identify those requirements that can be translated into formal statements

6. check for conflicts and inconsistency between requirements

7. change Requirements Description and Data Dictionary when conflicts exist and requirements have to be changed

9.1.2 Design

The aim of the object-oriented design process is to develop an abstract implementation concept for the system that has been specified by the analysis. During the analysis, the system's functionality is considered and specified almost exclusively from the global point of view of the user. In the operation model, too, which represents the most detailed specification of the analysis, effects are represented exclusively by changes of state on the already identified objects. No statements are made in which dynamic runs are responsible for these changes of state. The aim of design is to fully model and specify these dynamics.

The advantage of all object-oriented methods (including *Fusion$_B$*) is that they can be used with already existing static analysis models, which are enriched with additional information without invalidating the analysis models.

In the design phase, we look at the models built during the analysis phase and design a system that has the behaviour described in these models.

The first step in design is to formulate one object interaction graph for each system operation or operation schema. The information of the corresponding operation schema is used for this purpose. An object interaction graph is a dynamic model that maps the communication between the objects of the operation scheme by named message passing. This method enables interfaces to be partly fixed between classes of the objects used in the operation schema.

The second step is to enrich the output (Formal Description) of the consistency check between the Operation Model and the Object Interaction Model. The *Formal Description* is the specification of all classes of the system. One of the next steps towards a complete specification is to add the INIT operation to the classes. The class invariants, which have not yet been formulated, can be found in the formal statements of the system requirements, the Requirements Description, and added to the classes.

The third and fourth steps are analogous to steps two and three of Chapter 6.

9.2 Describing All Models and Their Role Within the Method

In this section, we describe the models and their role within the new method. Each model and its dependency on other models is motivated in a descriptive manner. The dependency of the models is shown graphically in Fig. 9.1.

The advantage of a descriptive view of the models over a graphical view is that one finds much more semantical information on the models and their role than one can find in a graphical view. Both views have their advantages and disadvantages.

9.2.1 Requirements Description

Goal: Identification of domain areas from the problem description, e.g. as potential actors, extraction and classification of requirements

Principles: Separation of different requirements types (system requirements and domain requirements)

Prerequisites: Problem description (is not part of the Fusion method)

Elements: Types of requirements, attributes of the requirements template

Impact: Preselection of actors for the Use Case Model and predefining use cases, finding candidates for class invariants and environment invariants

9.2.2 Use Case Model

Goal: Identifying functionality groups and their relationships, identifying the system boundary and actors through communication relationships

Principles: Identifying functionality groups and their relationships,
collection of individual scenarios to form a functionality group (use case),
decomposing actors, use cases and their behavioural structure of relationships, functionality group (use case)

Prerequisites: Requirements Description and Problem Description

Elements: Actor: type and name, gen/spec relationship between actors
system: assoziation between actor and use cases
use case: name, relationship between use cases: gen/spec, include and extend

Impact: Prestructuring of Timeline diagrams (classifying scenarios according to use cases), Operation Model (sends part), System Class Model (soft objects, mirroring of actor), Object Interaction Model (sender and receiver)

9.2.3 Domain Class Model

Goal:	Modelling the problem domain
Principles:	Abstraction: object to class, link to association refinement: aggregation and composition, Gen/Spec relationship modularization: Decomposition and static structure of relationship of global functionality
Prerequisites:	Requirements description and problem description
Elements:	Class: name, attribute, requirements link Association: name, attribute, attribute type, role, multiplicity (cardinality) gen/spec relationship, requirements links
Impact:	Fixation of the System Class Model as far as possible.

9.2.4 Timeline Model

Goal:	Identification of communication elements between actors and system (system operations and system events), identification of scenarios as sequences of action in time
Principles:	Modeling of scenarios (normal and exceptional cases), parameterization of system operations and system events, abstraction of system details
Prerequisites:	Use Case Model, Domain Class Model (only if parameterization (access of object(class) attributes))
Elements:	Actor and system instances, timelines for instances, System operation and system events, parameters, system-internal types
Impact:	Operation Model: Fixation of communication primitives and actor instances

9.2.5 Life Cycle Model

Goal:	Describes behaviour from a wider perspective on how the system communicates with its environmement. A life cycle expression defines the allowed sequence of interactions that a system may participate in over its lifetime.
Principles:	Modeling of sequences of interactions using path expressions and named abbreviations of subpaths, modelling top-down
Prerequisites:	Timeline Model
Elements:	Regular expressions, system operations and system events, operators, substitutions and operator precedence
Impact:	Operation Model and Object Interaction Model

9.2.6 System Class Model

Goal:	Modelling the system with all the system-internal classes and its environment.
Principles:	Abstraction: mirroring actors as "soft objects" in the system boundary, additional new class as controller for the system operation
Prerequisites:	Domain Class Model, Use Case Model
Elements:	Class: name, attribute, attribute type, system boundary: enclosing the system by a dotted line, association: name, attribute, attribute type, role, requirements links
Impact:	Operation Model, Object Interaction Model, Formal Model.

9.2.7 Operation Model

Goal: Modelling operation schemata describing changes of system state, which have been triggered by actors through system operations and their parameters

Principles: Description of changes of the system state using pre- and post-conditions in the style of Z or Object-Z (logical calculus)

Prerequisites: Timeline Model, System Class Model

Elements: Operation: name of system operation
Input Part: input parameter
Reads Part: objects, links and attributes that do not change the state of system.
Changes Part: objects, links and attributes that might change the state of system.
Sends Part: actors and system events
Precondition: defines the state of the system before the operation is executed.
Postcondition: defines the state of the system after the operation has been executed only if the precondition holds.

Impact: Object Interaction Model, Formal Model.

9.2.8 Object Interaction Model

Goal: Identifying all the communication flows between objects along links

Principles: Describing the message flow of a system operation between objects involved in the operation

Prerequisites: Operation Model and System Class Model

Elements: Actors, objects, links, procedure calls and sequencing of calls with decimal numbering system, guards.

Impact: Formal Description

9.2.9 Formal Description

Goal:	Specifying all objects of the system and its operations in a formal notation.
Principles:	For each class an INIT schema is included by examining the attributes of the state schema. Class invariants are included when possible. Candidates of variants are found in the Requirements Description.
Prerequisites:	Operation Model and System Class Model
Elements:	Notation of Object-Z (cf. [Smi00, DR00, Spi92])
Impact:	All models of the analysis, design and implementation phase

9.3 Modification of Some Modelling Elements

9.3.1 Modifying the Actor Symbols of the Use Case Model

The Use Case Model and specially the actors play an important role in modelling the behaviour of the system and its environment in an abstract way. The Use Case Model describes the interface of the system and its interacting partners. At the time of creating this model, we know what kind of actor is included and what kind of communication is taking place between actor and system. All this information should be expressed in the model by choosing the right actors.

An actor is a person or external software system or hardware device that plays a role in one or more interactions with the system. Actors are drawn as stick figures.

We distinguish between three types of actors:

An actor as external system (software or hardware) which delivers only input to the system:

Figure 9.2: An Actor with Input only

An actor as an external system (software) which delivers input and receives output in the form of values:

The third form is a person as an actor, which represents the graphical interface of the system, displayed on the screen of the input device of the computer on

Figure 9.3: An Actor with Input/Output

which the system is running and the person is interacting with the system:

Figure 9.4: A *Human* Actor

Actors and their association(s) represent the *environment interface* of the system. If we have access to the information of parameters (system operation) and arguments (system events) of the system interface, we should use this information by choosing the right actors. Note, that at this point in the modelling process we abstract from the type and name of input/output parameters an actor provides or receives. We prefer to show the direction of parameters (input/output) using the arrow symbol.

9.3.2   Modifying the Modelling Elements of the Domain Class Model

In order to link requirements to classes of the Domain Class Model, the modelling element class has been modified by dividing the second compartment, the attribute compartment, into two parts. The dividing line is a broken line. It will therefore not be in conflict with the UML class symbol, which has three compartments (name, attributes, methods).

Figure 9.5: Modification of the Class

The upper part of the compartment is for local attributes and the lower part for listing (linking) requirements identifiers and non-responsible statements identifiers as representatives of the requirements and non-responsible statements. As an example (cf. Fig. 7.6).

9.4 Consistency Checks

The consistency checks described here are based on the consistency check of Part ??. It is extended to the new models that are introduced to the new method.

The following are examples of simple consistency checks:

- All requirements listed in the Use Case Model and all requirements and non-responsible statements listed in the Domain Class Model must be in the Requirements Description.

- For each use case, at least one timeline diagram must exist. This is an example to enforce the use of the modelling element of a timeline diagram, which comes from a definition of a use case of the previous Use Case Model.

- All requirements, classes, associations and attributes used in the Operation Model must appear in the System Class Model. All predicates must be defined in the Data Dictionary. However, this does not rule out the addition of further attributes in the which must, of course, be consistent with the already existing ones.

- The boundary of the System Class Model is consistent with the Use Case Model. All actors defined in the Use Case Model have to appear in the System Class Model and Timeline Model.

- All system operations and their system events in the Timeline Model must appear in the Life Cycle Model.

- Each system operation in the Life Cycle Model has a corresponding operation schema.

- All identifiers in all models have entries in the Data Dictionary .

- Output of events of the Life Cycle Model and Operation Model must be consistent.

- Each class of the System Class Model must be represented in at least one object interaction graph.

- A systematic translation of the two main results of the process, the Operation Model and the Object Interaction Model, lead into the formal specification in Object-Z.

- Each association within the boundary of the System Class Model must be visible for the correspondent class of the reference graph.

Chapter 10

Conclusion

Starting from an existing software engineering method, we look at ways of eliminating what have been recognized as the method's deficiencies by modifying and extending it. Some of the main deficiencies are:

1. Nonexistence of concepts for supporting requirements engineering.

2. Missing unification of system models that reflects different views of the system.

3. Missing satisfying consistency rules to prove correctness between models.

Our remedy for these deficiencies is:

1. Requirements engineering is supported by the subprocess requirements determination. A new model and new modelling elements are included in the notation and a new consistency rule has been added to the existing ones. Furthermore, during the process requirements activities are present with new modelling elements and process elements.

2. A unified formal specification (on the basis of Object-Z) that is elicited from existing models.

3. Parts of the requirements are integrated into the formal specification.

4. Other models of the method are also modified because of the requirements process.

Our aim in this book has been to show that it is feasible to integrate parts of requirements engineering and formal specification into $Fusion_B$, and that it is possible to incorporate models- the Requirements Description and the Formal

Description into an existing object-oriented development method. New model and modelling elements are designed and integrated into the notation of *Fusion$_B$*.

The first extension to Fusion/UML deals with gathering, classifying and formalizing requirements for the system that is to be built. We have described the process of requirements determination. Emphasis has been placed on identifying the domains in the application field, extracting requirements and non-responsible statements from those domains, classifying requirements and, where possible, formalizing them.

One of the positive side effects of the Use Case Model, the decision about who is the actor, what are the use cases and how they communicate, has been set out in the requirements determination process. One other activity is linking the requirements to the other models of the method for the purpose of tracing. Modelling elements of existing models needed to be modified to enable requirements to be traced throughout the designed models, forwards and backwards.

Formalizing requirements in a logical language at this early stage of analysis also has an impact on the other models of the method. It helps to rethink requirements in terms of their meaning. The consistency check between models is widened by including requirements in consistency checks. With this approach, all the information regarding the problem is now part of the method, allowing it to be traced and checked throughout the process.

The clear and precise way of defining the requirements from the problem description and including this information in the method has some positive influence on the other models. They are more likely to be closer to the original requirements because they have been checked against them from the earliest stages of the analysis process.

The two most important models in Fusion for describing the system state are the Operation Model and Object Interaction Model. These two models are the ones that focus on the structure of the system. No other model in the method does this. The Operation Model describes the change state of the system which is triggered by the environment in a formal way.

The Object Interaction Model describes the change of state of the system by modelling the method flow between the objects of the system. It provides a consistency for the developed design: systematic translation of the two main results of the process, the Operation Model and the Object Interaction Model, into the formal description using Object-Z. We have shown that a mechanical and systematic translation is possible. Here, we have demonstrated a specific aspect of formalization. It is a pragmatic approach that requires more theoretical work in order to be generalized and to enable a more rigorous verification of system properties.

The result of the translation into Object-Z classes made it possible to enrich the Object-Z classes, which allowed a more complete specification with the INIT operation and identification of the class invariant from the formal statements of requirements determination , by examining the state variables of the class. The advantage of being able to choose the class invariants from the requirements description is that the formal statements of the requirements have been formulated in the same formal language as the Operation Model and Object-Z classes.

The extensions have been evaluated in two case studies. The first case study, DAISY-Soft, forms part of this book. The second case study has been the Automatic Teller Machine (ATM).

10.1 Future Work

This conceptional approach requires some theoretical work to provide a solid foundation, not only for the two models which have been presented but also for the other models of the methods, in particular the Life Cycle Model.

A method is only as good as the tool it provides for developing software. We have begun a student project to build a toolkit for the Fusion method. All project participants were students who were writing their Master's thesis. The project began by eliciting the requirements for a toolkit [Sah00]. Based on that requirements document, several students designed and implemented some models of the method, e.g. the Class Model and the System Class Model, the Use Case Model and the Timeline Model. However, our experience has shown that it is almost impossible to conduct such a project successfully. We have learned a lot from this experience. A new attempt would have to take place under different conditions. The design and implementation of a toolkit of this complexity should be carried out by a team of professionals and students, based on the results of the students' work. The work of the students is to be seen as a prototype of the toolkit.

Certain aspects of the design are not yet part of the method, e.g. the architecture of the system, the design of the graphical interface, the design of a data base, etc. Such extensions could be included in the process of the method, using the information from the already established models of the method.

Appendix A

The Case Study: DAISY-Soft

A.1 Problem Description

The public transport company of the city Belleville wants to install a DynAmic
Information SYstem called DAISY for all its underground stations.

The time table should have the terminus of all the next accepted trains and the
time interval in minutes of the estimated arrival time.

DAISY consists of different components:

- The Information Board for each station of a line , who can only show a
  certain amount of trains who are on the track.

- The Monitor Control System (MCS) that keeps control over the underground lines, trains, timetable and in case of emergency.

- The clock that frequently updates the time on stations and the trains.

- An embedded software system (*DAISY-Soft*) which must interact with components of its domain (actors). The task of DAISY-Soft is managing the
  different underground lines and of the running trains explicitly for the purpose of serving the timetables of trains with the correct and brand-new
  informations.

Informal description of DAISY-Soft:

DAISY-Soft treats the two directions of an underground line as two separate lines.
DAISY-Soft must have knowledge of the topology of the respective underground
line. A line as a software structure consists of a directed sequence of stations
with 2 unique stations, namely the start-terminal and the terminus. Lines and
Stations are objects with well defined attributes like the name of the station.

139

Moreover, the relationship between the stations and lines have to be designed in such a way which can themselves have attributes. Each line should be seen as a separate line independent of all the other lines. Each line has its own track which will not be used by any other lines.

Also DAISY-Soft must consider that each train will be established on the track by the Monitor Control System (MCS). Specific informations has to be made on the position of the train on the track and its state. Finally for each station a set of train information has to be administrated. A train-info has the identification of the train, as well as its position and expected arrival time. DAISY-Soft treats the two directions of an Underground line as two separate lines. It must have knowledge of the topology of the respective underground line. A line as a software structure consists of a directed sequence of stations with two unique stations, namely the start-terminal and the terminus. Lines and Stations are objects with well-defined attributes, like the name of the station. Moreover, the relationship between the stations and lines must be designed in such a way that each can in turn have attributes. Each line should be seen as a separate line, independent of all the other lines. Each line has its own track, which is not used by any other lines.

The driver is responsible for stopping and restarting the train at the stations, and is also responsible for opening and closing the train doors.

DAISY-Soft must also take into account that each train will be placed on the track by the Monitor Control System (*MCS*). Specific information on the position of the train on the track and its state must be recorded. Finally, for each station train information must be administered. The *Train-info* contains an identification of the train as well as its position and expected arrival time.

The administration of *Train-info* includes

- the generation of new info when the *MCS* establishes a train

- the deletion of info when the train leaves a station or reaches the terminus

- the updating of all info on the subsequent stations when a train leaves a station

If a train stops unexpectedly, all preceding trains are treated normally. All the following trains are given special treatment. Instead of the arrival times being displayed, a change has to be made in the form of a special announcement like "irregular train traffic" on the *Train-infos*.

Every clock at the underground station is updated by a central clock ensuring that all clocks show the same time.

At regular intervals, the station's *Information Board* fetches the train info from the system.

DAISY-Soft is not responsible for coding of the Information Board – it merely supplies the information – or for correcting or changing timetables, avoiding collisions, dealing with disasters or the like. Nor is it responsible for providing train informations in a specific order.

A.2 Requirements Definition

Extract the requirements of the domain area from the problem description, classify and formally describe them.

Domain:MCS

Req-Id	=	MCS_1
Type	=	Fact
Rational	=	MCS provides a unique train_number and a unique line_number when train is established at the start-terminal.
Formal	=	$\forall$ *trains* : *Train, lines* : *Line* $\mid$ $\exists t$: *trains, l* : *lines* $\bullet$ $(t, l) \in$ *Established*
Links	=	Domain Class Model

Req-Id	=	MCS_2
Type	=	Constraint
Rational	=	MCS must establish train at start-terminal on that line
Formal	=	
Links	=	Use Case Model

Req-Id	=	MCS_3
Type	=	Constraint
Rational	=	MCS stops train on track in case of emergency, initiates the generating of a special announcement for the Information Board and informs Driver of that train.
Formal	=	
Links	=	Use Case Model

Req-Id	=	MCS_4
Type	=	Constraint
Rational	=	Removes train at terminus when all passengers have left the train.
Formal	=	$\exists\, t : Train, l : Line, s : Station \mid s = l.terminus \wedge (t, l) \in Runs \setminus \{(t, l)\}$
Links	=	Use Case Model

Req-Id	=	MCS_5
Type	=	Fact
Rational	=	Has to remove train and informs Driver of the train.
Formal	=	
Links	=	Domain Class Model

Req-Id	=	MCS_6
Type	=	Fact
Rational	=	After an interrupt the Driver gets informed that journey can continue.
Formal	=	
Links	=	Domain Class Model

Domain: Driver

Req-Id	=	Driv_1
Type	=	Fact
Rational	=	Continues journey after regular stop at station.
Formal	=	
Links	=	Use Case Model

Req-Id	=	Driv_2
Type	=	Fact
Rational	=	Stops and continues journey of train on track (in communication with the MCS).
Formal	=	
Links	=	Use Case Model

Req-Id	=	Driv_3
Type	=	Fact
Rational	=	Makes announcement on the train during journey.
Formal	=	-
Links	=	Domain Class Model

Req-Id	=	Driv_4
Type	=	Fact
Rational	=	Opens and closes doors of train while train stops at the stations or between stations.
Formal	=	-
Links	=	Domain Class Model

Domain: Information Board

Req-Id	=	Info_1
Type	=	Fact
Rational	=	Has limit space for information on the Information Board.
Formal	=	-
Links	=	Domain Class Model

Req-Id	=	Info_2
Type	=	Fact
Rational	=	Asks for train information at regular intervals from DAISY-Soft.
Formal	=	
Links	=	Use Case Model

Req-Id	=	Info_3
Type	=	Fact
Rational	=	Updates train information on the Information Board every so often.
Formal	=	-
Links	=	Domain Class Model

Domain: Clock

Req-Id	=	Clock_1
Type	=	Fact
Rational	=	Updates continuously the time on Station, Train, MCS, and Information Board
Formal	=	-
Links	=	Domain Class Model

System Requirements

Req-Id	=	Sys_1
Type	=	System
Rational	=	The System must treat the two directions of an underground line as two separate lines.
Formal	=	$\exists\, undergound - line : Line \leftrightarrow Line \mid first(underground - line) \neq second(underground - line)$
Links	=	Use Case Model, Domain Class Model

Req-Id	=	Sys_2
Type	=	System
Rational	=	The system must treat two stations (start-terminal and terminus) as special stations on the line
Formal	=	$\exists\, s1 : Station, sn : Station, l : Line \bullet l.start - terminal = s1 \wedge l.terminus = sn$
Links	=	Use Case Model, Domain Class Model

Req-Id	=	Sys_3
Type	=	System
Rational	=	The system must know that all stations who follow the start-terminal on the line, these are the subsequent stations of that line.
Formal	=	
Links	=	Use Case Model, Domain Class Model

Req-Id	=	Sys_4
Type	=	System
Rational	=	The system must treat the start-terminal when train leaves the station different to the subsequent stations of the line.
Formal	=	
Links	=	Use Case Model, Domain Class Model

Req-Id	=	Sys_5
Type	=	System
Rational	=	The system shall update train information for all subsequent stations on the line when train leaves the station.
Formal	=	
Links	=	Use Case Model, Domain Class Model

Req-Id	=	Sys_6
Type	=	System
Rational	=	The system shall delete train information at the terminus when train has been disconnected at terminus (and only)
Formal	=	$terminus$: $Station, l$: $Line, t$: $traininfo \mid l.terminus = terminus \wedge (terminus, t) \in At\_display \bullet At\_display \rhd \{t\}$
Links	=	Use Case Model, Domain Class Model

Req-Id	=	Sys_7
Type	=	System
Rational	=	The system shall generate special information for the subsequent stations when train has been irregular stopped between two stations.
Formal	=	
Links	=	Use Case Model, Domain Class Model

Req-Id	=	Sys_8
Type	=	System
Rational	=	After the Information Board of the station has collected the information from the system, the system shall delete this information.
Formal	=	s : $Station, t$: $Traininfo \mid (s, t) \in At\_display \bullet At\_display \rhd \{t\}$
Links	=	Use Case Model, Domain Class Model

Non-responsible Statements

Req-Id	=	non-resp-1
Rational	=	All line-numbers are unique and are generated by the MCS.
Domain	=	MCS

Req-Id	=	non-resp-2
Rational	=	All train-numbers are unique and are generated by the MCS-System.
Domain	=	MCS

Req-Id	=	non-resp-3
Rational	=	Timetables of trains is under control of the MCS-System.
Domain	=	MCS

Req-Id	=	non-resp-4
Rational	=	DAISY-Soft is not responsible for the Information Boards.
Domain	=	InformationBoard

Req-Id	=	non-resp-5
Rational	=	DAISY-Soft is not responsible for train collision or any other catastrophes.
Domain	=	MCS

A.3   Use Case Model

The Use Case model describes the behavioural view of the system and its environment through the actors who are interacting with system. A Use Case abstracts from a the sequence of actions.

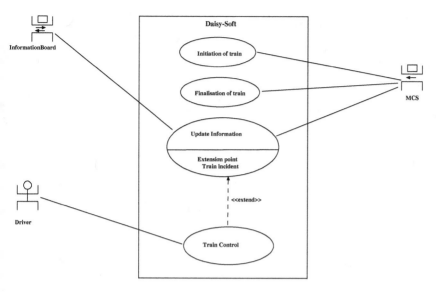

Figure A.1: Daisy Soft: Use Case Model

	Initialization of train	Finalization of train	Update Information	Train Control
MCS	MCS_2, Sys_1, Sys_2, Sys_4	MCS_4, Sys_6	MCS_3, Sys_7, Sys_3	
Driver				Driv_1, Sys_5, Driv_2, Sys_3,Sys_6
Information Board			Info_2, Sys_8	

Table A.1: Requirement links on use cases

A.4   Timeline Model

Each Timeline diagram refines a use case of the Use Case Model by its system operation and system events.

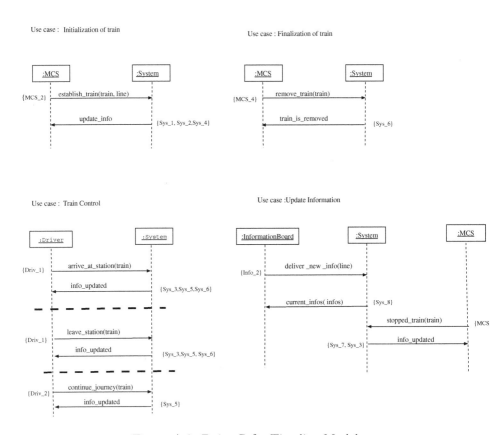

Figure A.2: Daisy Soft: Timeline Model

A.5 Domain Class Model

The Domain Class Model depicts the whole application domain of the system. It represents a static view of the domain.

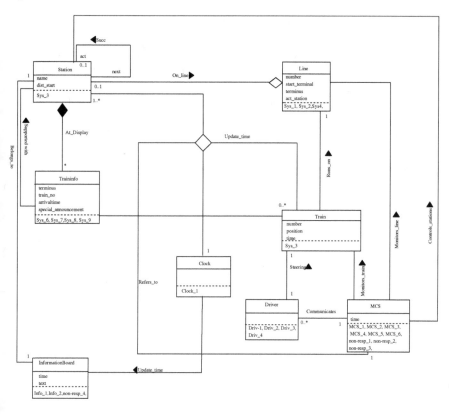

Figure A.3: Daisy Soft: Domain Class Model

A.6 Life Cycle Model

The Life Cycle Model describes the system in its whole from the point of system operation and system events.

Lifecycle DAISY-Soft $=$ (Initialize_train_journey; train_journey*; Finalize_train_journey ||Update_information)*

Initialize_train_journey $=$ establish_train; #infos_established

Train_journey	=	Train_leaves_station; (Arrives_at_station | Train_has_stopped)
Train_leaves_station	=	leave_station; #info_updated
Arrives_at_station	=	arrive_at_station; #info_updated
Train_has_stopped	=	train_stopped; #info_updated;continue_journey; #info_updated; arrive_at_station; #info_updated
Finalize_train_journey	=	remove_train;#train_is_removed
Update_information	=	deliver_new_infos; #infos_delivered

A.7 System Class Model

The System Class Model show the internal structure of the system and its actors which presents the communication environment.

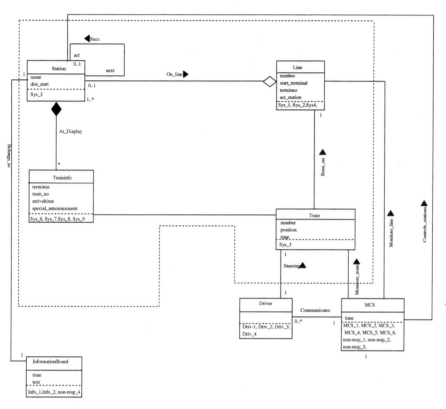

Figure A.4: Daisy Soft: System Class Model

A.8 The Operation Model

All the Operation Schemata in the Operation Model of DAISY-Soft are defined here. In the description part of each operation schema there is a short
textual description of what the operation does. The operations *establish_train,
arrive_at_station, leave_station, remove_train* describe a run beginning at the terminus by establishing the train on a track (line) and ending at the end terminal
by removing the train from the track. Between these two special terminals the
train arrives and leaves as many stations as there are on this particular line. The
operations *train_stopped, continue_journey* characterize the exceptional situation
which can occur during a run. Operation train_stopped is triggered by the MCS
because of an exceptional situation on the line or train. The system send a special
announcement to all subsequent stations on that line. When the stopped train
eventually continues its journey the Traininfos for the subsequent stations have
to be adjusted in a very similar manner as before to the new arrival times.

Operation	$=$	establish_train
Rational	$=$	MCD informs the system about having established the train of the specific line on the start_terminal.
Input	$=$	$train, line$
Reads	$=$	$act : Station$ **with** $act.name = l.start\_terminal, On\_line,$ $l : Line$ **with** $l.number = line$
Changes	$=$	$t : Train$ **new**, $info : Traininfo$ **new**, $Runs\_on, At\_display$
Sends	$=$	$: MCS : \{infos\_established\}$
Pre	$=$	$-$
Post	$=$	$t.number' = train$ $Runs\_on' = Runs\_on \cup \{(t, l)\}$ $t.position' = (act, 0)$ **is_sent** $\{info\_updated\} \wedge$ $(\forall s : Station \mid (s, l) \in On\_line \bullet$ $(info, s) \notin At\_display \wedge At\_display' = At\_display \cup \{(info, s)\}$ $info.train\_no' = train \wedge$ $(\exists i : Traininfo \mid (i, s) \in At\_display' \wedge$ $i.train\_no = train$ $i.arrival\_time = 0))$

Operation	=	arrive_at_station
Rational	=	When train gets into the station, the Traininfo of this station will be deleted. No traininfo of the subsequent stations will be updated.
Input	=	$train$
Reads	=	$act : Station$ **with** $Succ(first(t.position)) = act \wedge$ $(l, act) \in On\_line, Succ, \underline{t : Train}$ **with** $t.nr = train, \underline{l : Line}$
Changes	=	$\underline{info : Traininfo}$ **with** $(info, act.im) \in At\_display \wedge$ $info.train\_nr = train, At\_display, Traininfo$
Sends	=	$\underline{: Driver} : \{info\_updated\}$
Pre	=	—
Post	=	$At\_display' = At\_display \setminus (info, act)$ $t.position' = (act, 0)$ **is_sent** $\{info\_updated\}$

Operation	=	train_stopped
Rational	=	The MCS has stopped train between two stations. A special announcement has to be sent to all subsequent stations of this line.
Input	=	$train$
Reads	=	$\underline{act : Station}$ **with** $\{first(t.position)\}\!) = act$ $\underline{l : Line}$ **with** $(t, l) \in Runs\_on$ $On\_line, At\_display$
Changes	=	$\underline{t : Train}$ **with** $t.number = train, \underline{: Traininfo},$
Sends	=	$\underline{: MCS} : \{info\_updated\}$
Pre	=	—
Post	=	**is_sent** $\{info\_updated\} \wedge$ $t.pos' = (act, Succ(\!\{act\}\!)) \wedge$ $\forall \, s : Station \mid (s, l) \in On\_line \wedge s.dist\_start > act.dist\_start \bullet$ $\exists \, i : Traininfo \mid (i, s) \in At\_display \wedge i.train\_nr = train \bullet$ $i.arrivaltime' = special\_announcement$

Operation	=	leave_station
Rational	=	When the train leaves the station all arrival times of all train infos of a subsequent stations will be updated.

Input	=	$train, line$
Reads	=	$\underline{act : Station}$ **with** $first(t.position) = act$ $On\_line, Succ$ $\underline{l : Line}$ **with** $l.number = line$
Changes	=	$\underline{t : Train}$ **with** $t.train\_no = train,$ $At\_display, : \underline{Traininfo}$
Sends	=	$\underline{: Driver} : \{info\_updated\}$
Pre	=	—
Post	=	$t.position' = (act, Succ(act))$ **is_sent** $\{info\_updated\} \wedge$ $(\forall s : Station \mid (s, l) \in On\_line$ $s.dist\_act - act.dist\_start > 0 \wedge (s, act) \notin Succ \bullet$ $info.train\_no' = train \wedge$ $\quad (\exists i : Traininfo \mid (i, start) \in At\_display' \wedge$ $\qquad i.train\_no = train \bullet$ $\qquad\quad i.arrivaltime' = s.dist - act.dist\_start + sojourn))$ $(\exists s : Station \mid (s, l) \in On\_line \wedge (s, act) \in Succ \bullet$ $\quad (\exists i : Traininfo \mid (i, l.start\_terminal) \in At\_display' \wedge$ $\qquad i.train\_no = train \bullet$ $\qquad\quad i.arrivaltime' = s.dist - act.dist\_start))$

Operation	=	continue_journey
Rational	=	Train stopped unscheduled between two stations. MCS cleared th line and informed the Driver to continue the journey. All informatio (timetables) of the line has to be updated with the estimated time c arrival.

Input	=	$train$
Reads	=	$\underline{t : Train}$ **with** $t.train\_no = train,$ $\underline{act : Station}$ **with** $snd(t.pos) = act \wedge (act, l) \in On\_line,$ $\underline{l : Line}$ **with** $(t, l) \in Runs\_on, At\_display$
Changes	=	$: \underline{Traininfo},$
Sends	=	$\underline{: Driver} : \{info\_updated\}$
Pre	=	—
Post	=	**is_sent** $\{info\_updated\} \wedge$ $\forall s : Station \mid (s, l) \in On\_line \wedge s.dist\_start > act.dist\_start \bullet$ $\quad \exists i : Traininfo \mid (i, s) \in At\_display \wedge i.train\_no = train \bullet$ $\qquad i.arrivaltime' = s.dist\_start - act.dist\_start + retentic$

Operation	=	remove_train
Rational	=	MCS informs the system about removing train from the terminus.
Input	=	*train*
Reads	=	$\underline{act : Station}$ **with** $act = l.terminus \wedge (l, act) \in On\_line,$ $\underline{l : Line}$ **with** $l.number = line$
Changes	=	$\underline{t : Train}$**delete with** $t.number = train \wedge (t, l) \in Runs\_on,$
Sends	=	$\underline{: MCS} : \{train\_is\_removed\}$
Pre	=	–
Post	=	$Runs\_on' = Runs\_on \setminus \{(t, l)\}$ **is_sent** $\{train\_is\_removed\}$

Operation	=	deliver_new_infos
Rational	=	The Information board requests every 30 secs the train info of the station.
Input	=	*station, line*
Reads	=	$\underline{act : Station}$ **with** $act = station \wedge (l, s) \in On\_line,$ $\underline{l : Line}$ **with** $l.number = line,$ $info : Traininfo$ **with** $(act, info) \in At\_Display$
Changes	=	$\underline{t : Train}$ **delete with** $t.number = train \wedge (t, l) \in Runs\_on,$
Sends	=	$\underline{: Informationboard} : \{updateinfo(info)\}$
Pre	=	–
Post	=	*noeffect* **is_sent** $\{updateinfo(info)\}$

A.8.1 Translating Operationschemata to an Object-Z Class

We now translate all operation schemata to one Object-Z class. All "basic types" which are used in state schema of the class "System" are declared as data structures.

$Report ::= info\_updated \mid Train\_has\_been\_removed \mid infos\_established \mid infos\_delivered$

_____ *System_OP* _____

> *On_line* : *Station* ↔ *Line*
> *l* : *Line*
> *t* : *Train*
> *info* : *Traininfo*
> *act_station* : *Station*
> *Succ* : *Station* ↔ *Station*
> *At_display* : $\mathbb{P}$ *Traininfo* ↔ *Station*
> *Runs_on* : $\mathbb{P}$ *Train* ↔ *Line*
>
> ___ *establish_train* _____
> $\Delta(t, At\_display, info)$
> *train?*, *line?* : $\mathbb{N}$
> *m!* : *Report*
> _____
> *train?* = *t.number* $\wedge$ *line?* = *l.number*
> *act_station* = *l.start_terminal*
> *t.position′* = (*act_station*, *no_station*)
> (*act_station*, *l*) $\in$ *On_line* $\wedge$ (*t*, *l*) $\in$ *Runs_on*
> *m!* = *infos_established*
> ($\forall$ *s* : *Station* | (*s*, *l*) $\in$ *On_line* •
> $\wedge$ (*s*, *info*) $\notin$ *At_display* $\wedge$ *At_display′* = *At_display* $\cup$ {(*s*, *info*)}
> *info.train_no′* = *train?*
> ($\exists$ *i* : *TrainInfo* | (*s*, *i*) $\in$ *At_display* $\wedge$ *i.train_no* = *train?* •
> *i.time_of_arrival′* = 0))

_arrive_at_station_

$\Delta(t)$
$train? : \mathbb{N}$
$m! : Report$

$train? = t.number$
$act\_station = second(t.position)$
$t.position' = (act\_station, 0)$
$(act\_station, l) \in On\_line \wedge (t, l) \in Runs\_on$
$m! = info\_updated$
$(\forall \ s : Station \mid (s, l) \in On\_line \ \bullet$
$\wedge \ (s, info) \notin At\_display \wedge At\_display \cup \{(s, info)\}$
$info.train\_no' = train?$
$(\exists \ i : Traininfo \mid (s, i) \in At\_display \wedge i.train\_no = train? \ \bullet$
$i.time\_of\_arrival' = 0))$

_leave_station_

$\Delta(t, At\_display)$
$train? : \mathbb{N}$
$m! : Report$

$train? = t.number$
$act\_station = first(t.position)$
$m! = info\_updated$
$t.position' = (act\_station, Succ(\!|\{act\_station\}|\!))$
$act\_station = l.start\_terminus \Rightarrow$
$(\exists \ i : Traininfo \mid (s, i) \in At\_display \wedge i.train\_no = train? \ \bullet$
$At\_display' = At\_display \setminus \{(s, info)\}$
$(\forall \ s : Station \mid (s, l) \in On\_line \wedge (s.dist\_start - act.start\_dist > 0$
$\wedge \ (s, act) \notin Succ \ \bullet$
$(\exists \ i : Traininfo \mid (s, i) \in At\_display \wedge i.train\_no = train? \ \bullet$
$i.time\_of\_arrival' = s.dist\_start - act.dist\_start + sojourn))$
$(\exists \ s : Station \mid (s, l) \in On\_line \wedge (s, act) \in Succ \ \bullet$
$(\exists \ i : Traininfo \mid (s, i) \in At\_display \wedge i.train\_no = train? \ \bullet$
$i.time\_of\_arrival' = s.dist\_start - act.dist\_start))$

_train_stopped_

$train? : \mathbb{N}$
$m! : Report$

$train? = t.number \wedge (l, t) \in Runs\_on$
$act\_station = second(position)$
$\forall \ s : Station \mid (s, l) \in On\_line \wedge s.dist\_start > act.dist\_start \ \bullet$
$\exists \ i : Traininfo \mid (s, i) \in At\_display \wedge i.train\_no = train? \ \bullet$
$i.time\_of\_arrival' = special\_announcement$
$m! = info\_updated$

```
┌─ continue_journey ──────────────────────────────────────────────
│  train? : ℕ
│  m! : Report
│ ┌───────────────────────────────────────────────────────────────
│ │ train? = t.number ∧ second(t.position) = act_station
│ │ (act_station, l) ∈ On_line ∧ (t, l) ∈ Runs_on
│ │ m! = info_updated
│ │ ∀ s : Station | (s, l) ∈ On_line ∧ s.dist_start − act.dist_start > 0 •
│ │ ∃ i : Traininfo | (s, i) ∈ At_display ∧ i.train_no = train? •
│ │ i.time_of_arrival′ = s.dist_start − act_station.dist_start + sojourn
```

```
┌─ remove_train ──────────────────────────────────────────────────
│  Δ(t, Runs_on)
│  train? : ℕ
│  m! : Report
│ ┌───────────────────────────────────────────────────────────────
│ │ act_station = l.terminus ∧ (act, l) ∈ On_line
│ │ train? = t.number ∧ (t, l) ∈ Runs_on
│ │ Runs_on′ = Runs_on \ {(t, l)}
│ │ m! = Train_has_been_removed
```

```
┌─ deliver_new_infos ─────────────────────────────────────────────
│  line? : ℕ
│  s : Station?
│  info! : ℙ Traininfo
│  m! : Report
│ ┌───────────────────────────────────────────────────────────────
│ │ line? = l.number ∧ (s, l) ∈ On_line
│ │ ∧ (t, l) ∈ Runs_on
│ │ Runs_on′ = Runs_on \ {(t, l)}
│ │ info! = dom(At_display)
│ │ m! = infos_delivered
```

```
┌─ Station ──────────────────────┐    ┌─ Train ────────────────────┐
│ ┌──────────────────────────────┤    │ ┌──────────────────────────┤
│ │ name : Name                  │    │ │ position : Station × Station
│ │ dist_start : ℕ               │    │ │ number : ℕ
└─┴──────────────────────────────┘    └─┴──────────────────────────┘
```

```
┌─ Line ─────────────────────────┐    ┌─ Traininfo ────────────────┐
│ ┌──────────────────────────────┤    │ ┌──────────────────────────┤
│ │ start_terminal, terminus : Station  │ │ time_of_arrival : ℕ
│ │ stations : seq Station       │    │ │ special_announcement : Report
│ │ number : ℕ                   │    │ │ train_no, line_no : ℕ
└─┴──────────────────────────────┘    └─┴──────────────────────────┘
```

A.9   Object Interaction Model

For each operation schema of the DAISY-Soft system there is a corresponding object interaction graph. An Object interaction graph describes the dynamic message flow between objects involved in the system operation.

Figure A.5: Object interaction for establish_train

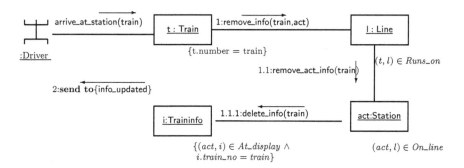

Figure A.6: Object interaction for arrive_at_station

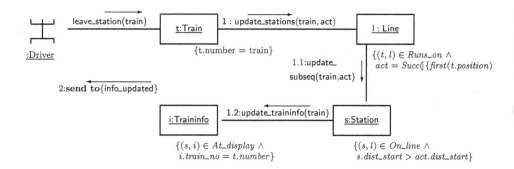

Figure A.7: Object interaction for leave_station

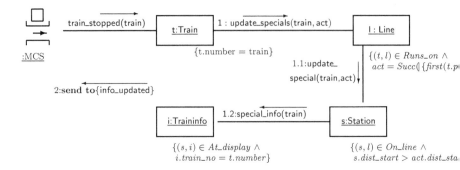

Figure A.8: Object interaction for train_stopped

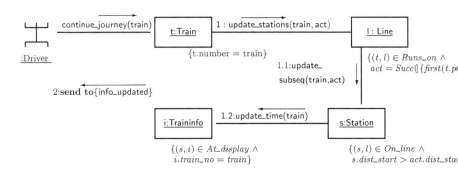

Figure A.9: Object interaction for continue_journey

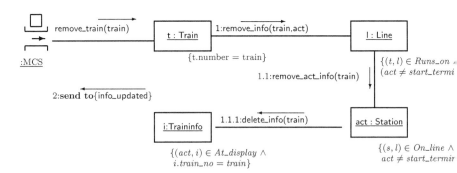

Figure A.10: Object interaction for remove_train

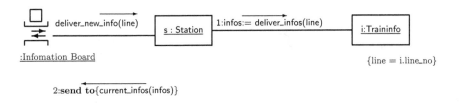

Figure A.11: Object interaction for deliver_new_info

A.9.1 Translating Objectinteraction Model to Object-Z Classes

Report ::= info_updated | Train_has_been_removed | infos_established | infos_delivered

```
┌─ Line ──────────────────────────────────────────────────────────────
│
│  ┌──────────────────────────────────────────────────────────────
│  │  start_terminal, terminus : Station
│  │  stations : ℙ Station
│  │  trains : ℙ Train
│  │  number : ℕ
│  └──────────────────────────────────────────────────────────────
│
│  ┌─ remove_train ──────────────────────────────────────────────
│  │  Δ(trains)
│  │  train? : ℕ
│  │  m! : Report
│  ├──────────────────────────────────────────────────────────────
│  │  ∃ t : trains | t ∃ trains ∧ t.number = train? •
│  │  trains' = trains \ {t}
│  │  m! = Trains_has_been_removed
│  └──────────────────────────────────────────────────────────────
│
│  ┌─ establish ─────────────────────────────────────────────────
│  │  Δ(trains)
│  │  train? : ℕ
│  │  line? : ℕ
│  │  m! : Report
│  ├──────────────────────────────────────────────────────────────
│  │  ∃ t : trains | t ∉ trains •
│  │  t.number' = trains?
│  │  t.act' = start_terminal
│  │  trains' = trains ∪ {t}
│  │  m! = infos_established
│  └──────────────────────────────────────────────────────────────
│
│  establish_train ≙ [s : stations, m! : Report | m! = infos_established] •
│                        establish; ⋀ s.create_infos
│  update_stations ≙ ⋀[s : stations),  train? : ℕ, act? : Station |
│                        s.dist_start > act?.dist_start] • s.update_subseq
│  update_specials ≙ ⋀[s : stations,  t?train : ℕ, act? : Station |
│                        s.dist_start > act?.dist_start] • s.update_special
│
└──────────────────────────────────────────────────────────────────────
```

Train

$l : Line$
$position : Station \times Station$
$act : Station$
$number : \mathbb{N}$

---

update_position

$\Delta(position)$
$train? : \mathbb{N}$

$train? = self.number$
$position' = position \oplus \{(second(position), Succ(second(position)))\}$

$arrive\_at\_station \;\hat{=}\; [\Delta(l)\; train? : \mathbb{N}, m! : Report \mid train? = self.number$
$\qquad\qquad m! = info\_updated] \bullet l.remove\_info$

$leave\_station \;\hat{=}\; [\Delta(l)\; train? : \mathbb{N}, m! : Report \mid train? = self.number$
$\qquad\qquad m! = info\_updated] \bullet update\_position \parallel l.update\_stations$

$train\_stopped \;\hat{=}\; [\Delta(l)\; train? : \mathbb{N}, m! : Report \mid train? = self.number$
$\qquad\qquad m! = info\_updated] \bullet l.update\_specials$

$continue\_journey \;\hat{=}\; [\Delta(l)\; train? : \mathbb{N}, m! : Report \mid train? = self.number$
$\qquad\qquad \wedge\; m! = info\_updated] \bullet update\_position \parallel l.update\_stations$

```
┌─ Station ────────────────────────────────────────────────────────────
│
│  ┌─────────────────────────────────────────────────────────────────
│  │ name : Name
│  │ dist_start : ℕ
│  │ infos : ℙ Traininfo
│  └─────────────────────────────────────────────────────────────────
│
│  ┌─ create_info ───────────────────────────────────────────────────
│  │ Δ(infos)
│  │ train? : ℕ
│  │ line? : ℕ
│  ├─────────────────────────────────────────────────────────────────
│  │ ∃ info : infos | info ∉ infos •
│  │ info.train_no′ = train?
│  │ info.line_no′ = line?
│  │ infos′ = infos ∪ {info}
│  └─────────────────────────────────────────────────────────────────
│
│  ┌─ remove_act_info ───────────────────────────────────────────────
│  │ Δ(infos)
│  │ train? : ℕ
│  ├─────────────────────────────────────────────────────────────────
│  │ ∃ info : infos | info.train_no = train? ∧ info ∈ infos •
│  │ infos′ = infos \ {info}
│  └─────────────────────────────────────────────────────────────────
│
│  deliver_new_info ≙ [line? : ℕ, info! : infos; m! : Report | m! = current_infos ∧
│                          info!.line_no = line?] • info!.deliver_infos
│  update_special ≙ [info : infos, train? : ℕ | info ∈ infos ∧ info.train_no = train?] •
│                          info.special_info
│  update_subseq ≙ [info : infos, train? : ℕ | info ∈ infos ∧ info.train_no = train?] •
│                          info.update_traininfo
└──────────────────────────────────────────────────────────────────────
```

```
┌─ Traininfo ──────────────────────────────────────────────
│ ┌──────────────────────────────────────────────────────
│ │ time_of_arrival : ℕ
│ │ special_announcement : Report
│ │ train_no, line_no : ℕ
│ └──────────────────────────────────────────────────────
│
│ ┌─ update_special_info ────────────────────────────────
│ │ Δ(special_announcement, time_of_arrival)
│ │ train? : ℕ
│ ├──────────────────────────────────────────────────────
│ │ self.train_no = train? time_of_arrival' = 0
│ │ special_announcement' = "reasonsfordelay"
│ └──────────────────────────────────────────────────────
│
│ ┌─ update_traininfo ───────────────────────────────────
│ │ Δ(time_of_arrival)
│ │ train? : ℕ
│ ├──────────────────────────────────────────────────────
│ │ self.train_no = train?
│ │ time_of_arrival' = time_of_arrival + rentation
│ └──────────────────────────────────────────────────────
└──────────────────────────────────────────────────────────
```

A.10 Formal Description

$Report ::= info\_updated \mid Train\_has\_been\_removed \mid infos\_established \mid infos\_delivered$

____ *Line* _____

$start\_terminal, terminus : Station$
$stations : \mathbb{P}\ Station$
$trains : \mathbb{P}\ Train$
$number : \mathbb{N}$

$start\_terminal \neq terminus \land start\_terminal \in stations \land terminus \in stations$

____ *remove_train* _____

$\Delta(trains)$
$train? : \mathbb{N}$
$m! : Report$

$\exists\ t : trains \mid t \exists\ trains \land t.number = train? \bullet$
$trains' = trains \setminus \{t\}$
$m! = Trains\_has\_been\_removed$

____ *establish* _____

$\Delta(trains)$
$train? : \mathbb{N}$
$line? : \mathbb{N}$
$m! : Report$

$\exists\ t : trains \mid t \notin trains \bullet$
$t.number' = trains?$
$t.act' = start\_terminal$
$trains' = trains \cup \{t\}$
$m! = infos\_established$

$establish\_train \mathrel{\widehat{=}} [s : stations, m! : Report \mid m! = infos\_established] \bullet$
$\qquad\qquad\qquad establish;\ \bigwedge s.create\_infos$

$update\_stations \mathrel{\widehat{=}} \bigwedge [s : stations, train? : \mathbb{N}, act? : Station \mid$
$\qquad\qquad\qquad\quad s.dist\_start > act?.dist\_start] \bullet s.update\_subseq$

$update\_specials \mathrel{\widehat{=}} \bigwedge [s : stations,\ t?train : \mathbb{N}, act? : Station \mid$
$\qquad\qquad\qquad\quad s.dist\_start > act?.dist\_start \bullet s.update\_special$

___ *Train* _____

┌───
│ $l : Line$
│ $position : Station \times Station$
│ $act : Station$
│ $number : \mathbb{N}$
├───
│
│ ___ INIT _____
│ $act = \varnothing \wedge position = (0,0) \wedge number = 0$
│
│ ___ *update_position* _____
│ $\Delta(position)$
│ $train? : \mathbb{N}$
│ ─────────────────────────────────
│ $train? = self.number$
│ $position' = position \oplus \{(second(position), Succ(second(position)))\}$
│
│ $arrive\_at\_station \mathrel{\hat{=}} [\Delta(l)\; train? : \mathbb{N}, m! : Report \mid train? = self.number$
│ $\qquad\qquad m! = info\_updated] \bullet l.remove\_info$
│
│ $leave\_station \mathrel{\hat{=}} [\Delta(l)\; train? : \mathbb{N}, m! : Report \mid train? = self.number$
│ $\qquad\qquad m! = info\_updated] \bullet update\_position \parallel l.update\_stations$
│
│ $train\_stopped \mathrel{\hat{=}} [\Delta(l)\; train? : \mathbb{N}, m! : Report \mid train? = self.number$
│ $\qquad\qquad m! = info\_updated] \bullet l.update\_specials$
│
│ $continue\_journey \mathrel{\hat{=}} [\Delta(l)\; train? : \mathbb{N}, m! : Report \mid train? = self.number$
│ $\qquad\qquad \wedge\; m! = info\_updated] \bullet update\_position \parallel l.update\_stations$
└───

___ *Station* _____

> _____
> $name : Name$
> $dist\_start : \mathbb{N}$
> $infos : \mathbb{P}\ Traininfo$
> _____
>
> ___ $INIT$ _____
> $dist\_start = 0 \land \forall\, i : infos \bullet i.INIT$
> _____
>
> ___ *create_info* _____
> $\Delta(infos)$
> $train? : \mathbb{N}$
> $line? : \mathbb{N}$
> _____
> $\exists\, info : infos \mid info \notin infos \bullet$
> $info.train\_no' = train?$
> $info.line\_no' = line?$
> $infos' = infos \cup \{info\}$
> _____
>
> ___ *remove_act_info* _____
> $\Delta(infos)$
> $train? : \mathbb{N}$
> _____
> $\exists\, info : infos \mid info.train\_no = train? \land info \in infos \bullet$
> $infos' = infos \setminus \{info\}$
> _____
>
> $deliver\_new\_info \mathrel{\widehat{=}} [line? : \mathbb{N}, info! : infos;\ m! : Report \mid m! = current\_infos \land$
> $\qquad\qquad\qquad\qquad info!.line\_no = line?] \bullet info!.deliver\_infos$
> $update\_special \mathrel{\widehat{=}} [info : infos, train? : \mathbb{N} \mid info \in infos \land info.train\_no = train?] \bullet$
> $\qquad\qquad\qquad\qquad info.special\_info$
> $update\_subseq \mathrel{\widehat{=}} [info : infos, train? : \mathbb{N} \mid info \in infos \land info.train\_no = train?] \bullet$
> $\qquad\qquad\qquad\qquad info.update\_traininfo$

```
┌─ Traininfo ─────────────────────────────────────────────────┐
│                                                              │
│  ┌───────────────────────────────────────────────────────┐  │
│  │ time_of_arrival : ℕ                                    │  │
│  │ special_announcement : Report                          │  │
│  │ train_no, line_no : ℕ                                  │  │
│  └───────────────────────────────────────────────────────┘  │
│                                                              │
│  ┌─ INIT ────────────────────────────────────────────────┐  │
│  │ train_no = line_no = time_of_arrival = 0               │  │
│  └───────────────────────────────────────────────────────┘  │
│                                                              │
│  ┌─ update_special_info ─────────────────────────────────┐  │
│  │ Δ(special_announcement, time_of_arrival)               │  │
│  │ train? : ℕ                                             │  │
│  ├───────────────────────────────────────────────────────┤  │
│  │ self.train_no = train? time_of_arrival' = 0            │  │
│  │ special_announcement' = "reasonsfordelay"              │  │
│  └───────────────────────────────────────────────────────┘  │
│                                                              │
│  ┌─ update_traininfo ────────────────────────────────────┐  │
│  │ Δ(time_of_arrival)                                     │  │
│  │ train? : ℕ                                             │  │
│  ├───────────────────────────────────────────────────────┤  │
│  │ self.train_no = train?                                 │  │
│  │ time_of_arrival' = time_of_arrival + rentation         │  │
│  └───────────────────────────────────────────────────────┘  │
│                                                              │
└──────────────────────────────────────────────────────────────┘
```

A.11 Data Dictionary

The Data Dictionary of DAISY-Soft as presented here is not complete. The complete
Data Dictionary would be to

Data Dictionary

Name	Type	Description	Source
MCS_1	requirement	domain	Domain Class Model
MCS_2	requirement	domain	Use Case Model, Domain Class Model, Timeline Model, System Class Model-Timeline Model, System Class ModelTimeline Model, System Class Model
MCS_3	requirement	domain	Use Case Model, Domain Class Model, Timeline Model, System Class Model
MCS_4	requirement	domain	Use Case Model, Domain Class Model, Timeline Model, System Class Model
MCS_5	requirement	domain	Use Case Model, Domain Class Model, Timeline Model, System Class Model
MCS_6	requirement	domain	Use Case Model, Domain Class Model, Timeline Model, System Class Model
Driv_1	requirement	domain	Use Case Model, Domain Class Model, Timeline Model, System Class Model
Driv_2	requirement	domain	Use Case Model, Domain Class Model, Timeline Model, System Class Model

Name	Type	Description	Source
Driv_3	requirement	domain	Domain Class Model
Driv_4	requirement	domain	Domain Class Model
Info_1	requirement	domain	Domain Class Model
Info_2	requirement	domain	Use Case Model,Domain Class Model, Timeline Model, System Class Model
Info_3	requirement	domain	Domain Class Model
Clock_1	requirement	domain	Domain Class Model
Sys_1	requirement	system	Use Case Model,Domain Class Model, Timeline Model, System Class Model
Sys_2	requirement	system	Use Case Model,Domain Class Model, Timeline Model, System Class Model
Sys_3	requirement	system	Use Case Model,Domain Class Model, Timeline Model, System Class Model
Sys_4	requirement	system	Use Case Model,Domain Class Model, Timeline Model, System Class Model
Sys_5	requirement	system	Use Case Model,Domain Class Model, Timeline Model, System Class Model

Name	Type	Description	Source
Sys_6	requirement	system	Use Case Model, Domain Class Model, Timeline Model, System Class Model
Sys_7	requirement	system	Use Case Model, Domain Class Model, Timeline Model, System Class Model
Sys_8	requirement	system	Use Case Model, Domain Class Model, Timeline Model, System Class Model
non-resp_1	requirement	statement	Domain Class Model
non-resp_2	requirement	statement	Domain Class Model
non-resp_3	requirement	statement	Domain Class Model
non-resp_4	requirement	statement	Domain Class Model
non-resp_5	requirement	statement	Domain Class Model
Station	class	train arrives and leaves station. At the station the train information are announced.	Domain Class Model, Timeline Model, System Class ModelSystem Class Model Operation Model Object Interaction Model Formal Description
Line	class	is one line of an underground-line	Domain Class Model
TrainInfo	class	has all information of one train that is at moment running on the line per station. When train enters a station the information of that train is deleted.	Domain Class Model
Clock	class	The clock represents the time which has to be frequently updated. Is not part of the system.	Domain Class Model

Name	Type	Description	Source
Train	class	Train represents the drive from the start-terminal to the terminus.	Domain Class Model, Timeline Model, System Class Model
InformationBoard	class, actor	Is the forum on the station to display the expected arrival time of train and direction	Domain Class Model, Timeline Model, System Class ModelUse Case Model, System Class Model,Operation Model, Object Interaction Model, Formal Description
Driver	class,actor	Is the person who is driving the train on the line	Domain Class Model, Timeline Model, System Class ModelUse Case Model, Timeline Model,Operation Model
MCS	class,actor	It is the Monitor Control System of the Underground lines.	Domain Class Model, Timeline Model, System Class ModelUse Case Model, Timeline Model,Operation Model,
name	attribute	Name of a station of a underground line	Domain Class Model, System Class Model
train_no	attribute	Identification number of a train	Domain Class Model
arrivaltime	attribute	Estimated time of the train arrival in a station	System Class Model
special announcement	attribute	For special announcement of train traffic	System Class Model
number	attribute	Number of stations on the line	Domain Class Model
dist_startbhf	attribute	Timing from start terminal to current station	Domain Class Model
position	attribute	Has the current position of the train	Domain Class Model

Name	Type	Description	Source
start_terminal	attribute	start terminal of the line	Domain Clas Model
terminus	attribute	terminus of the line	Domain Clas Model
number	attribute	Number of stations on the line	Domain Clas Model
Belongs_to	assoziation	Every station belongs to a line	Domain Clas Model
Runs_on▶	assoziation	Zug fhrt auf einer Strecke (Assoziation).	Domain Clas Model
Monitors_train▶	assoziation	MCS monitors all train in the underground network	Domain Clas Model
Monitors_line▶	assoziation	MCS monitors all underground lines in the underground network	Domain Clas Model
Controls_stations▶	assoziation	MCS controls every station on he line	System Clas Model
Communicates	assoziation	Driver and MCS informs each other on exceptional situations and when entering and leaving a station.	Domain Clas Model
Update_time	assoziation	Time on Information Board, Train, Traininfo , Station gets frequently updated	Domain Clas Model
Supported_with▶	assoziation	The Information Board gets information of running trains	System Clas Model
Initialization_of_train	use case	MCS initializes train with number at the start-terminal	Use Case Model
Finalization_of_train	use case		Use Case Mode Timeline Model
Update Information	use case		Use Cas Model,Timeline Model
Train Control	use case		Use Cas Model,Timeline Model
leave_station	system operation	Train leaves station. The arrival train have to be calculated and send to all subsequent stations of the line.	Timeline Mode Life Cycle Mode Operation Mode Object Inter action Mode Formal Descrip tion

Name	Type	Description	Source
arrive_at_station system operation		Train has arrived at station. Train info of the train has to be deleted at the current station	Timeline Model, Life Cycle Model, Operation Model, Object Interaction Model, Formal Description
deliver_new_info	system operation	New train information of a particular station is wanted by the Information Board.	Timeline Model, Life Cycle Model, Operation Model, Object Interaction Model, Formal Description
continue_journey	system operation	Train continues journey. Train information have to be updated at all subsequent stations.	Timeline Model, Life Cycle Model, Operation Model, Object Interaction Model, Formal Description
remove_train	system operation	Train has reached its destination, the terminus. Information at the terminus has to be removed.	Timeline Model, Life Cycle Model, Operation Model, Object Interaction Model, Formal Description
establish_train	system operation	Train has been set up at the start-terminal. The train information only at the start terminal has to be initiated.	Timeline Model, Life Cycle Model, Operation Model, Object Interaction Model, Formal Description
stopped_train	system operation	Train gets stopped between stations. Special announcement has to be generated.	Timeline Model, Life Cycle Model, Operation Model, Object Interaction Model, Formal Description

Name	Type	Description	Source
info_updated	system event	Train info at station is updated.	Timeline Model, Life Cycle Model, Operation Model, Object Interaction Model, Formal Description
current_infos	system event	the up to date train infos	Timeline Model, Life Cycle Model, Operation Model, Object Interaction Model, Formal Description
establish_new_train	method	Next train is set on the line at the start-terminal.	Object Interaction Model, Formal Description
create_infos	method	Train info for the set up train is generated for all stations of the line.	Object Interaction Model, Formal Description
remove_info	method	Infos of several trains are collected by the Information Board of the station and can be removed from the TrainInfo.	Object Interaction Model, Formal Description
remove_act_info	method	Actual_info of a train at the station can be deleted because train left station.	Object Interaction Model, Formal Description
delete_info	method		Object Interaction Model, Formal Description

Appendix B

Syntax Description of the $Fusion_B$ Models

B.1 Graphical Notation

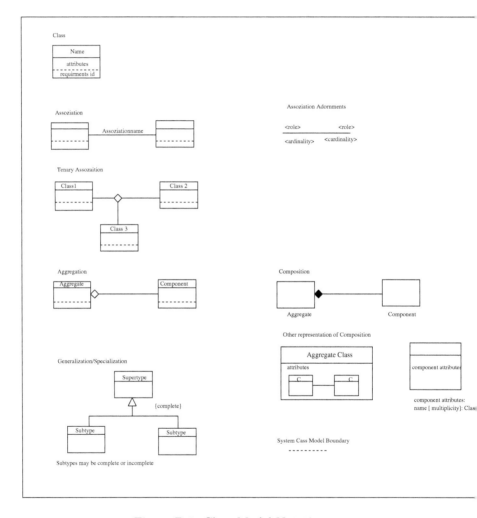

Figure B.1: Class Model Notation

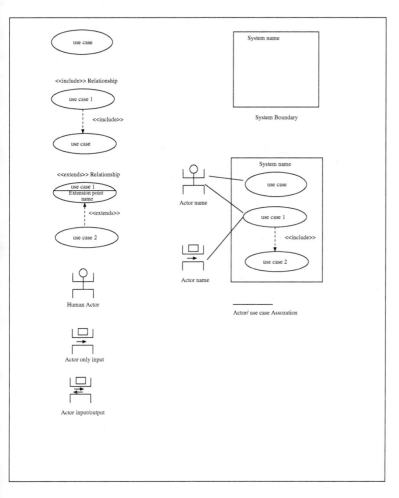

Figure B.2: Use Case Model Notation

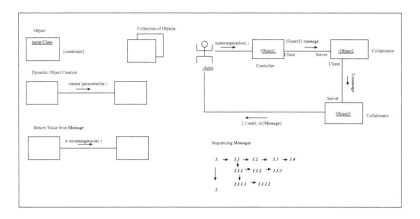

Figure B.3: Object interaction graph Notation

B.2   Notes on the Structure of the Syntactic Meta Language

Several Fusion models are defined using a number of syntactic rules. Each rule consists of a Left-Hand Side (LHS) and a Right-Hand Side (RHS). The syntactic notion of the LHS is explained by (derived from) the syntactic notions on the RHS. The LHS and RHS are separated by the syntactic meta symbol ::=. Each RHS consists of a set of alternatives or exactly one alternative and is concluded with the meta symbol.. Alternatives are separated by the meta symbol |. An alternative is a sequence of syntactic units. Syntactic units are either syntactic notions or terminal symbols (tokens) or bracket expressions of the language being tokens - also called terminal symbols - of the language are rendered in a particular typeface (**bold** or *italics*) that differs from the meta language's normal typeface.

All the notions of an alternative are separated by blanks. To avoid ambiguity, the underline symbol _ is therefore used instead of a blank within a syntactic unit.

Bracket expressions are either repetitions, options or underlinings. Repetition is expressed by the meta symbols (and) followed by a meta symbol *. The meaning, as usual, is the formation of the empty sequence or nonempty sequences, of arbitrary length, of copies of the bracket contents, separated by blanks.

An option brackets a sequence of syntactic units using the meta symbols [and] . This notation is a combination of two alternatives, one of which contains bracketed units and the other of which does not.

For all the languages described here, the terminal symbols are described once. Notions that denote the terminal symbols are identified by the suffix symbol. There are syntactic notions that are not deduced from terminal symbols (e.g. identifiers). Note: further deduced notions are written in lower-case letters. All other non-terminal symbols begin with an upper-case letter.

An underlining brackets a sequence of syntactic units with the meta symbols (and), which is preceded by the keyword **underline** (without blanks). It has the following meaning: all terminal derivations of the syntactic notions contained in the bracket are continuously (not separately) underlined.

B.3   Terminal Symbols

alternative_symbol	::=	||
becomes_symbol	::=	:=
close_brace_symbol	::=	}

close_bracket_symbol	::=	]
close_square_symbol	::=	]
close_symbol	::=	)
colon_symbol	::=	:
comma_symbol	::=	,
comprehension_symbol	::=	•
cr_symbol	::=	*carriage return*
element_symbol	::=	∈
equal_symbol	::=	=
greater_symbol	::=	>
greaterequal_symbol	::=	≥
hashmark_symbol	::=	#
hide_symbol	::=	\
integer_type_symbol	::=	ℤ
intersection_symbol	::=	∩
less_symbol	::=	<
lessequal_sybol	::=	≤

minus_symbol	::=	-
not_element_symbol	::=	$\notin$
not_equal_symobol	::=	$\neq$
open_brace_symbol	::=	{
open_bracket_symbol	::=	[
open_square_symbol	::=	[
open_symbol	::=	(
parallel_symbol	::=	|
period_symbol	::=	.
plus_symbol	::=	+
power_symbol	::=	$\mathbb{P}$
prime_symbol	::=	$\prime$
product_symbol	::=	$\times$
repetition_symbol	::=	$*$
semicolon_symbol	::=	;
subset_symbol	::=	$\subset$
subsetequal_symbol	::=	$\subseteq$

union_symbol	::=	$\cup$
vertical-line_symbol	::=	$\mid$

B.4   Requirements Description

Requirements_definition	::=	Requirement_list| Non-responsible_list.
Requirement_list	::=	Requirement | Requirement Requirement_list.
Requirement	::=	Requirement_Identifier Requirement_type Description [Formal_statement] Model_links .
Requirement_Identifier	::=	**Id** equal_symbol Domain_abbreviation underscore sym
Domain_abbreviation	::=	identifier.
Requirement_type	::=	**Type** equal_symbol **Fact** | **Constraint** | **System**.
Description	::=	**Rational** equal_symbol Verbal_description .
Formal_statement	::=	**Formal** equal_symbol Predicate.
Predicate	::=	$\forall$ Declaration_list $\bullet$ Simple_Condition | $\exists$ Declaration_list $\bullet$ Simple_Condition | Simple_Condition | {Textual_Description}.
Simple_Condition	::=	Equivalence| Implication| Disjunction | Conjunction | Negation |

ReL_Expr |
Predicate. [1]

Model_links	=	**Links** equal_symbol Model_list.
Model_list	=	Model_name | Model_name comma_symbol Model_list.
Model_name	::=	Use Case Model | Domain Class Model | Timeline Model | System Class Model | Data Dictionary.
Non-responsible_ list	::=	Non-responsible| Non-responsible Non-responsible_ list.
Non-responsible	::=	Non-responsible_Identifier Description Responsible .
Non-responsible_Identifier	::=	**Id** equal_symbol **non-resp** underscore_ symbol digits.
Responsible	::=	**Domain** equal_symbol Domain_name.

B.5   Life-CycleModel

lifecycle_model	::=	**lifecycle** System_name equal_symbol Path_expression [List_of_Abbrev_def].
Path_expression	::=	Path_expression parallel_symbol Path_expression | Alternative.
Alternative	::=	Alternative alternative_symbol Alternative| Sequence.

---

[1]These expressions have already been defined in Section **??**

Sequence	::=	Sequence semicolon_symbol Sequence |
		Iteration.
Iteration	::=	Primitive asterisk_symbol |
		Primitive plus_symbol |
		Option.
Option	::=	open_square_symbol Option_expression close_square_sy
Option_expression	::=	Path_expression |
		Primitive.
Primitive	::=	Systemoperation |
		hashmark_symbol Systemevent|
		Abbreviation | open_symbol Path_expression close_sym
List_of_Abbrev_def	::=	List_of_Abbrev_def Abbrev_definition |
		Abbrev_definition.
Abbrev_definition	::=	identifier equal_symbol Path_expression.
System_name	::=	identifier.
Systemevent	::=	identifier.
Systemoperation	::=	identifier.

B.6   Operation schema

Operation_Schema	::=	Operation_Naming
		[Operation_Description]
		[Input_Part]
		[State_Part]

[System_Event_Part]

[Precondition]

Postcondition.

Operation_Naming	::=	**Operation** = Identifier.
Operation_Description	::=	**Description** = Textual_Description.
Input_Part	::=	**Reads** = RItemlist.
State_Part	::=	**Changes** = CItemlist.
System_Event_Part	::=	**Sends** = Actor: { Systemevent}.
Precondition	::=	**Pre** = Predicate.
Postcondition	::=	**Post=** Predicate.
RItemlist	::=	RItemlist , RItem | RItem.
RItem	::=	[**supplied**] Argument.
CItemlist	::=	CItemlist , CItem | CItem.
CItem	::=	Variable | Object **new** | Object **delete** | Object **transient**.
Systemevent	::=	Identifier.
Predicate	::=	$\forall$ Declaration_list • Simple_Condition | $\exists$ Declaration_list • Simple_Condition | **let** let_Def (;let_Def)* • Predicate |

| | | Simple_Condition \| |
| | | {Textual_Description}. |

Simple_Condition	::=	Equivalence|
		Implication|
		Disjunction |
		Conjunction |
		Negation |
		ReL_Expr |
		Predicate.

| Equivalence | ::= | Equivalence $\equiv$ Implication \| |
| | | Implication. |

| Implication | ::= | Disjunction $\Rightarrow$ Implication \| |
| | | Disjunction. |

| Disjunction | ::= | Disjunction $\vee$ Implication \| |
| | | Disjunction. |

Conjunction	::=	Conjunction $\wedge$ ReL_Expr |
		ReL_Expr |
		Predicate_sequence.

| Predicate_sequence | ::= | Predicate_sequence **cr_symbol** Predicate \| |
| | | Predicate**cr_symbol** Predicate. |

| Negation | ::= | $\neg$ Simple_Condition. |

| ReL_Expr | ::= | Expression ReL_Op Expression [(ReL_Op Expression)*] \| |
| | | (Predicate). |

| ReL_OP | ::= | $\in$ \| Infix_ReL_Op |

| Infix_ReL_Op | ::= | $\neq$ \| $\notin$ \| $\subseteq$ \| $\subset$ \| $>$ \| $\leq$ \| $\geq$ \| $>$. |

| let_Def | ::= | Variable_Name $= =$ Expression. |

Declaration_List	::=	Basic_Decl (; Basic_Decl)*.
Basic_Decl	::=	Decl_Name (, Decl_Name)* : Type_Expr | Basic_Decl vertical_line-symbol Simple_Condition.
Expression	::=	**if** Predicate **then** Expression **else** | (**let** let_Def (; let_Def)* • Expression) | Type_Expr | Simple_Expr.
Type_Expr	::=	$\mathbb{P}$ Type_Expr | Type_Expr × Type_Expr (× Type_Expr)* | (Type_Expr) | Basic_Type.
Basic_Type	::=	Identifier | $\mathbb{Z}$.
Simple_Expr	::=	Simpe_Expr In_Fun Simple_Expr | Simple_Expr | unsigned_decimal_Integer | Set_Expr | (Simple_Expr (, Simple_Expr)*) | Argument | Qualified_attribute | Qualified_attribut Decoration | (Simple_Expr) | **no effect** | **is_sent** { systemevent }.
Decoration	::=	*I*.
In_Fun	::=	+ | − | ∪ | \ | *.
Set_Expr	::=	{ [Expression (, Expression)*] } | { Declaration_list • Expression }.
Argument	::=	Identifier | Variable.
Variable	::=	Object | Qualified_attribute | Type_name **with** Condition.
Object	::=	<u>object_name:Type_name</u> |

| | | :Type_name \| |
| | | Decorated_object. |

Decorated_object	::=	Object **{ new }** |
		Object **{ delete }** |
		Object **{ transient }**.
Qualified_attribute	::=	Object.attribute_name.
Type_name	::=	class_name |
		association_name.
cr_symbol	::=	Carriage return.
vertical_line-symbol	::=	|

B.7   Messages

Message_label	::=	[Guard_condition]
		Sequence_expression colon_symbol
		[return_value becomes_symbol] message_na⯈
		[open_bracket_symbol Argument_list
		close_bracket_symbol].
Guard_condition	::=	open_square_symbol predicate
		square_close_symbol |
		repetiton_symbol [open_square_symbol
		Iteration_spec close_square_symbol].
Iteration_spec	::=	iteration_expression.
Argument_list	::=	Argument [comma_symbol Argument_list]*

Argument	::=	actual_parameter_expression.
Sequence_expression	::=	integer [period_symbol Sequence_expression].
Return_value	::=	identifier [comma_symbol identifier]*.

B.8   Classinterface

CID	::=	**class** name [Superclass_Part]
		Feature_Part
		endclass name .

Feature_Part	::=	[Attribute_Part] [Methode_Part].

Attribute_Part	::=	**attribute** Attribute_Liste |
		attribute Attributelist Attribute_Part.

Attribute_List	::=	Attribute (comma_symbol Attribute)*.

Attribute	::=	[Mutability] Identifier colon_symbol Type |
		[Mutability] [Binding] Identifier colon_symbol
		[Visibility][**col**] class_name.

Type	::=	basic_type_name |
		Enumeration |
		Structured_Type.

Structured_Type	::=	[type_name] (Type (comma_symbol ,Type)*).

Enumeration	::=	(Identifier (| Identifier)*).

Mutability	::=	**const** |
		var.

Binding	::=	**bound** |

		unbound.
Visibility	::=	**shared** | **exclusive**.
Method_Part	::=	**method** Method_List | **method** Method_List Method_Part.
Method_List	::=	Method (, Method)*.
Method	::=	Identifier ([Parameter_List]) [Return_Part].
Parameter_List	::=	Parameter (,Parameter)*.
Parameter	::=	Parameter_name [: Type].
Return_Part	::=	**:** basic_type_name | **:** Structured_Type| .
Superclass_Part	::=	**behaves_like** Superclass_name (comma_symbol Superclass_name)*.

Appendix C

Requirements Artefacts for a *Fusion$_B$* Tool

A Requirement template consists of the following entries:

Identifier	:	unique number
Name	:	name of requirement
Type	:	{Constraint | Fact | System}
Rational	:	description
	:	
	:	
Creater	:	
Date	:	
	:	{complete | deferred | inconsistent | conflict}
	:	
	:	
Link to other models	:	
Link to Data Dictionary	:	
	:	either name or project number

There are entries, which have to be filled out by the creator, some will be filled out automatically by the system and others are optional. Those which have to be filled out by the user are marked in red. Those which are inscribed by the system are marked in blue and the optional entries are marked in green.

When masking out all optional entries than the template looks as follows, that is what the creator would see:

Identifier	:	unique number
Name	:	name of requirement
Type	:	{Constraint | Fact | System}

Rational	:	description
Creator	:	
Date	:	
Link to other models	:	
Link to Data Dictionary	:	

A Non-Responsible template has the following entries:

Identifier	:	unique number
Name	:	name of Non-responsible Statement
Rational	:	description
Domain	:	name of domain to which the Non-resp. belongs to
	:	
Creator	:	
Date	:	
	:	projects or subsystems
Link to Data Dictionary	:	
	:	either name or project number

Bibliography

[Ale64]   C. Alexander. *Notes on the synthesis of form*. Havard University Press, 1997 edition, 1964.

[Ale77]   C. Alexander. *A Pattern Language*. Oxford University Press, 1977.

[Ale79]   C. Alexander. *The Timeless Way of Building*. Oxford University Press, 1979.

[Baa03]   S. Baase. *A Gift of Fire*. Prentice Hall, Pearson Education, 2003.

[Bar97]   R.L. Barber. Comparison of Electrical Engineering of Heaviside's Times and Software Engineering of Our Times. *IEEE Annals of the History of Computing*, 1997.

[Bar02]   I. K. Bary. *An Introduction to Requirements Engineering*. Addison Wesley, pearson education limited edition, 2002.

[BCK98]   L. Bass, P. Clements, and R. Kazman. *Software Architecture in Practice*. Addision-Wesley, 1998.

[BD01]   M. Broy and E. Denert, editors. *Pioneers and their Contribution to Software Engineering*. Springer, Bonn, 2001.

[BH04]   E. Berki, E.and Georgiadou and M. Holcombe. Requirements Engineering and Process Modelling in Software Quality Management - Towards a Generic Process Metamodel. *Software Quality Journal*, 12(3):265–283, September 2004.

[BI96]   B. Boehm and H. In. Identifying Quality - Requirement Conflicts. *IEEE Software*, 1996.

[BK00]   M. Bittner and W. Koch. Objektorientierte Analyse und Design. Die Fusion-Methode unter Verwendung von UML. Script, 2000.

[BK01]   M. Bittner and W. (ed.) Koch. Softwareentwicklung mit Komponenten. Technical report, Forschungsberichte der Fakultät IV - Elektrotechnik und Informatik, 2001, 11, Technische Universität Berlin, 2001.

[BK03]   M. Bittner and F. Kammüller. Translating Fusion/UML to Object-Z. In R. K. Gupta, editor, *Proceedings "First ACM and IEEE International Conference on Formal Methods and Models (MEMOCODE'03)"*, 2003.

[Boe86]   B.W. Boehm. A Spiral Model of Software Development and Enhancement. *IEEE Computer*, 20(9):43–58, 1986.

[Böh02]   R. Böhmert. Konsistenzüberprüfung zwischen einzelnen Modellen der Fusion-Methode. Master's thesis, Fakultät Elektrotechnik und Informatik, 2002.

[Boo94]   G. Booch. *Object-oriented Analysis and Design with Applications*. Benjamin Cummings, second edition, 1994.

[Bro87]   F.P. Brooks. No silver bullet: essence and accidents of software engineering. *IEEE Computer*, 20(4):10–19, April 1987.

[Bro95]   F.P. Brooks. *The Mythical Man-Month, Essays on Software Engineering*. Addison-Wesley, anniversary edition, 1995.

[Cea94]   D. Coleman and et al. *Object-Oriented Development The Fusion Method*. Prentice-Hall, 1994.

[Che76]   P. Chen. The Entity Relationship Model - Towards a Unified View of Data. *ACM Transaction on Database Systems*, pages 9–36, 1976.

[CYll]   P. Coad and E. Yourdon. *Object-Oriented Analysis*. 1991 Prentice-Hall.

[Dav93]   A. M. Davis. *Software Requirements, Objects, Functions and States*. Prentice Hall, first edition, 1993.

[DB01]   J. Derrick and E. Boiten. *Refinement in Z and Object-Z – Foundations and Advanced*. Springer FACIT, 2001.

[Dem79]   T. Demarco. *Structured Analysis and System Specification*. Yourdon Press, Prentice Halls Building, Englewood Cliffs, 1979.

[DR00]   R. Duke and G. Rose. *Formal Object-Oriented Specification Using Object-Z*. Macmilian Press, 2000.

[DW98]   D. F. D'Souza and A. C. Wills. *Objects, Components and Frameworks with UML, The Catalysis Approach*. Addison-Weseey, 1998.

[Eps97]   R. G. Epstein. *The Case of the Killer Robot From Design to Disaster: An exploration in Computer Ethics*. John Wiley & Sons, Inc., 1997.

[Fai85]   R. Fairley. *Software Engineering Concepts*. McGraw-Hill, 1985.

[Fau97]   S. R. Faulk. Software requirements: A tutorial. In R. H. Thayer and M. Dorfman, editors, *SOFTWARE REQUIREMENTS ENGINEERING*, pages 128 –149. IEEE Computer Society Press, 2 edition, 1997.

[Fea05]   R. E. Filman and et al. *Aspect Oriented Software Development*. Addision-Wesley, 2005.

[GF95]   O. Gotel and A. Finkelstein. Contribution Structures. In *Proceedings of the Second IEEEInternational Symposium on Requirements Engineering (RE'95)*, pages 100–107, 1995.

[GF97]   O. Gotel and A. Finkelstein. Extended Requirements Traceability: Results from an Industrial Case Study. In *Proceedings of the Third IEEE- International Symposium on Requirements Engineering (RE'97)*, pages 169–179. IEEE Computer Society Press, 1997.

[GKJ95]   B. Groth, W. Koch, and S. Jähnichen. Software und Softwaretechnik. In R. Wilhelm, editor, *Identität der Informatik*. C.H. Beck Verlag, 1995.

[GL93]   J. Goguen and Ch. Linde. Techniques for Requirements Elicitation. In Stephen Fickas and Anthony Finkelstein, editors, *Proceedings, Requirements Engineering '93*, pages 152–164. IEEE Computer Society, 1993.

[Gra98]   I. Graham. *Requirements Engineering and Rapid Development*. Addison Wesley, 1998.

[Gut01]   J. V. Guttag. *Abstract Types Then and Now*, page 444. Springer, 2001.

[Har87]   D. Harel. STATECHARTS: A Visual Formalism for Complex Systems. *Science of Computer Programming*, 8:231–274, 1987.

[HPW98]   P. Haumer, K. Pohl, and K. Weidenhaupt. Requirements Elicitation and Validation with Real World Scenarios. *IEEE Transaction on Software Engineering*, 1998.

[HS97]   M. Heisel and J. Souquieres. Methodological support for requirements elicitation and formal specification. *ACM Transactions on Software Engineering and Methodology*, 1997.

[Hut94]   T.F. Hutt, editor. *Object Analysis and Design - Description of Methods*. John Wiley, 1994.

[Jac83]   M. Jackson. *System Development*. Prentice-Hall, 1983.

[Jac95]   M. Jackson. *Software Requirements and Specifications*. Addison-Wesley, 1995.

[Jac99]   M. Jackson. Problem Analysis Using Small Problem Frames. *South African Computer Journal*, 1999.

[Jac00]   M. Jackson. *Problem Frames. Analyzing and structuring software development problems*. Addision-Wesley, 2000.

[JBR98]   I. Jacobson, G. Booch, and J. Rumbaugh. *The Unified Software Development Process*. Addison-Wesley, 1998.

[Jea92]   Jacobsen and et al. *Object-Oriented Software Engineering*. Addison Wesley, 1992.

[KHB04]   N. Kühn, W. Hoffmann, M.and Weber, and M. Bittner. Requirements for Requirements Management Tools. In 12th *Requirements Engineering Conference 2004*, 2004.

[KS97]   G. Kotonya and I. Sommerville. *Requirements Engineering , Processes and Techniques*. John Wiley & Sons, 1997.

[Lar97]   C. Larman. *Applying UML and Patterns, An Introduction to Object-Oriented Analysis and Design*. Prentice Hall, 1997.

[LK95]   P. Loucopoulos and V. Karakostas. *System Requirements Engineering*. The McGraw-Hill International Series in Software Engineering. McGraw-Hill Book Company, 1995.

[Mac96]   L. A. Macaulay. *Requirements Engineering*. Springer Verlag, 1996.

[Mac01]   L. A. Maciaszek. *Requirements Analysis and System Design*. Addison Wesley, Pearson Education, 2001.

[McD91]   J.A. McDermid. *Software Engineer's Reference Book*. Butterworth-Heinemann, 1991.

[Mey88]   Bertrand Meyer. *Object-Oriented Software Construction*. Prentice Hall, 1988.

[Mor90]   C.C. Morgan. *Programming from Specifications*. Prentice Hall, 1990.

[NR69]   P. Naur and B. Randell, editors. *Report on a conference sponsored by the NATO SCIENCE COMMITTEE , Garmisch Germany 7th to 11th October 1968*. Scientific Affairs Division NATO Belgium, 1969.

[oEE90]   Institute of Electrical and Electronics Engineers, editors. *IEEE Standard Computer Dictionary: A Compilation of IEEE Standard Computer Glossaries*, 1990.

[OMG99]   OMG. UML – Notation Guide Version 1.3. Technical report, June 1999.

[Par71]   D. L. Parnas. Information Distribution Aspects of Design Methodology. *Proceedings of IFIP Congress 1971*, 1971.

[Par94]   D. L. Parnas. Software Ageing. *IEEE Transaction on Software Engineering*, 1994.

[Pre01]   Roger Pressmann. *Software Engineering: A Practitioner's Approach*. McGraw-Hill, 2001.

[PS94]   B. Pagel and H. Six. *Software Engineering, Band 1: Die Phasen der Softwareentwicklung*. Addison-Wesley, 1994.

[PST91] B. Potter, J. Sinclair, and D. Till. *An Introduction to Formal Specification and Z*. Prentice Hall, 1991.

[RBP⁺91] J. Rumbaugh, M. Blaha, W. Premerlani, F. Eddy, and W. Lorensen. *Object-Oriented Modeling and Design*. Prentice-Hall, 1991.

[Ros77] D. Ross. Structured Analysis: A Language for Communicating Ideas. *IEEE Transaction on Software Engineering*, 3(1):16–34, 1977.

[RS77] D. Ross and K. Schomann. Structured Analysis for Requirements Definition. *IEEE Transactions on Software Engineering*, SE-3(1), 1977.

[RSE95] B. Ramesh, C Stubbs, and M. Edwards. Lessons Learned from Implementing Requirements Traceability. *Journal of Defense Software Engineering*, pages 11–15, 1995.

[Sah00] B. Sahin. Anforderungsanalyse für die Werkzeugunterstützung der Methode FUSION und Entwurf einer Benutzungsschnittstelle. Master's thesis, Technische Universität Berlin, 2000.

[San05] George Santayana. *The Life of Reason: Or, The Phases of Human Progress, Introduction and Reason in Common Sense* . Scribner's, 1905.

[SBS03] A. Strohmeier, T. Baar, and S. Sendall. Applying FONDUE to Specify a Drink Vending Machine. *Electronic Notes in Theoretical Computer Science*, 2003.

[Sch02] B. Schoeller. Ein Repository für die Verwaltung von Requirements. Master's thesis, Technische Universität Berlin, 2002.

[SEI95] Carnegie Mellon University Software Engineering Institute. *Capability Maturity Model: Guidelines for Improving the Software Process*. Addison Wesely, 1995.

[SM98] A. Sutcliffe and N. Maiden. The Domain Theory for Requirements Engineering. *IEEE Transaction on Software Engineering*, 1998.

[Smi00] G. Smith. *The Object-Z Specification Language*. Kluwer Academic Publisher, second edition, 2000.

[Som01] I. Sommerville. *Software Engineering, sixth edition*. Addison-Wesley, 2001.

[Spi92] J.M. Spivey. *The Z Notation, A Reference Manual*. Prentice-Hall, second edition, 1992.

[SS96] J. Siddiqi and M. C. Shekaran. Requirements Engineering:"The Emerging Wisdom". *IEEE Software*, 13(2), March 1996.

[SS97] I Sommerville and P. Sawyer. *Requirements Engineering, A good practice guide*. John Wiley & Sons, 1997.

[SS00]   S. Sendall and A Strohmeier. UML Based Fusion Analysis Applied to a Bank Case Study. In *UML'99 - The Unified Modeling Language. Beyond the Standard*, pages 278–291. Springer , LNCS, 2000.

[Szy98] C. Szyperski. *Component Software: Beyond Object-oriented Programming.* Addison-Wesley, 1998.

[TD97]   R. Thayer and M. Dorfman, editors. *SOFTWARE REQUIREMENTS EN-GINEERING.* IEEE Computer Society Press, second ed. edition, 1997.

[Web93] Merriam Webster. *Merriam Webster's collegiate dictionary.* Merriam-Webster, Incorporated, 10th edition, 1993.

[Zav97] P. Zave. Classification on Research Efforts in Requirements Engineering. *ACM Computing Surveys*, 29(4), 1997.

[ZJ97]   P. Zave and M. Jackson. Four dark corners of requirements engineering. *ACM Transactions of Software Engineering and Methodology..*, 6(1):1–30, 1997.

Index

www.ingramcontent.com/pod-product-compliance
Lightning Source LLC
LaVergne TN
LVHW022310060326
832902LV00020B/3376